GW01159257

Self-Dis

The Key to Personal Success

Self-Discipline
The Key to Personal Success

By

Megan Daniels

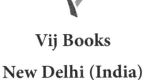

Vij Books

New Delhi (India)

Published by

Vij Books
(*An Imprint of Vij Books India Pvt Ltd*)
(Publishers, Distributors & Importers)
4836/24, 3rd Floor, Ansari Road
Delhi – 110 002
Phone: 91-11-43596460
Mobile: 98110 94883
e-mail: contact@vijpublishing.com
www.vijbooks.in

ISBN: 978-81-97691-34-8 (PB)

Contents

Introduction

The Unyielding Path to Success: Mastering Self-Discipline

Success, in all of the manners, is seldom a result of only luck or fortune. It is accumulated myriad of purposefully aimed activities, which are guided by one's clear objectives that he has sworn never to give up on. The entire list of goals, the chief goal is that it would a tool the success of each of them be a discipline in control of oneself. You cannot accomplish them which is even the most aspiring ones, however. People must be able to know the genuine idea of self-control, why and how they may become better with the help of it at the end, decide on which methods are the most effective ones, and develop the necessary skill of persistence.

The self-restraint is a tool that leads the tread to the ride of the goal, thereby making the individuals to stay focused on their objectives, even in the most adverse conditions. The self-discipline is not the matter of overt frustration or tight frameworks; on the contrary, it is the cultivation of the true understanding and the link between one's activities and the core point. The disciplined individual is aware that success takes hard work and that the path to it is often a difficult one that requires the constancy of one's will. Still, it is him/her who does the self-discipline, the one who gains the will to face it.

Indeed, the self-discipline comes about in standing out strikingly for its own sake, when we juxtapose it with any other things. When one fights back through self-control, the chance may not come into effect. You may fly from duties, too, thanks to the allure of the short-gain, of falling the main purpose which is the long-term gratifications in the case of a lack of or of minimal power of appeal. This concentration dropping can turn you into an

1

unfocused person full of missed opportunities where talent is wasted. Hence, it's not a simple tool for success, but it's a protection measure against failure. It makes the individual take the final step of achieving the goal, but not of falling down.

To envisage what self-discipline truly constitutes, one should be able to get rid of its outer-layered image as merely a kind of self-restraint. At the very heart of self-discipline is control, that is, the driving force of the will—the will that drives one to act as an independent agent, and the will that embodies the faculties of reason, responsibility, and morality within oneself. It is the ability to regulate oneself so that one's choices and behavior may lead to the achievement of long-term objectives rather than the immediate satisfaction of desires. It's not just willpower but a whole changed mind, getting into the center of the problems and changing the conscious level.

A disciplined mind is that which, after undergoing a process that trains the mind to concentrate on what truly matters, is now able to implement the training it has gone through by remembering the potential one may link up with when both energy and time are used productively and by not wasting either the mentioned resources on pursuits that do not promote the main aim. This self-discipline is mastered through the regular practice of shaping the fleeting intentions into stable habits. These once the habits are in place, it becomes a foundation where the successful continuum is not just feasible but also inevitable.

The import of consistency in the drive to success can never be gainsayed. It is the very element that brings discipline into fruition. It is not sufficient to be more disciplined every now and then, or it is not right to be when it is comfortable only. Through formidable practice through self-discipline, one can develop the necessary strength to reach success on their own. It involves remaining true to the objectives you have set no matter how gradually they are proceeding to come up with advanced obstacles that may seem impossible to overcome. And through it all, consistency will be the factor through which every small effort will accumulate and these will slowly but surely assemble into the much-desired objective.

2

Furthermore, besides the specific aims that self-discipline implies, self-discipline brings about a number of benefits that reach further beyond. It gives rise to self-respect and personal integrity, since individuals trust in themselves and their capacity to keep their promises are a result of learning. Along with that, it is associated with resilience, as people with self-discipline deal with challenge and discomfort more efficiently. Thus, through times, it evolves into a more organized life process that can add to one's life experience on every lane.

On the one hand, it is obvious that self-discipline is not merely a factor that one has the choice of not considering, but instead, this characteristic is actually one of the keys to success. Those who master self-discipline would wield a superior tool which they would apply to any part of their life, including from career success to personal growth. They are taught the lesson that achievement is not only a function of good fortune or talent, but also the infrangible result of regimented, disciplined practice extended over a period. This way, self-discipline comes from manipulation of one's mind and the key to personal success, which frees the way for a future filled with accomplishing and fulfillment.

Chapter 1

The Foundation of Self-Discipline

This chapter sets the stage for understanding self-discipline by exploring its fundamental concepts, psychological underpinnings, and its critical role in achieving success. Each subheading within this chapter will delve into specific aspects of self-discipline, providing readers with a comprehensive understanding of its importance and how it operates within the human experience.

Self-Discipline: The Bedrock of Personal Mastery

People have widely promoted the concept of self-discipline as the fundamental factor of both personal and professional success for years. It is like a secret power that lets one sustain the resistance to immediate temptations and proceed on a long-term path. In order to fully grasp the importance of self-discipline, one has to find out more about how it grew, get to know its basic principles, and clearly separate it from other related concepts like self-control, motivation, and determination. Thus, we can gain a comprehensive understanding of the mechanism that lies behind self-discipline and we will know why it is a gem for success.

This is a well-documented term, as word "self-discipline" has a rich etymological history that defines its essence nowadays. The word "discipline" is a product of Latin origin, coming from "disciplina," which in Latin means instruction or training. In the etymology of Latin, the root of "discipline" is said to be "discere," which is used to indicate learning. Initially, the word discipline was used to refer to the process through which one was trained to follow what was considered proper or to keep the certain set of standards. The training was typically done through the military or religious communities, where following the rules strictly was the main thing. As time went by, the concept of discipline was broadened to incorporate self-discipline, where an individual has a dual existence as both the teacher and the student, setting personal standards and adhering to them without external enforcement.

Self-discipline is also about prescription to personal or communal norms. It requires setting clear benchmarks for behavior and performance, whether these norms are self-adopted or imposed by social ones, professional codes of conduct, or valuing personal norms. By following standards, one ensures that his/her actions are stable and congruent with their goals. A framework is formed within which disciplined behavior can be cultivated, thus, stability and guidance are both provided. Inasmuch as compliance with self-discipline principles has to be chosen by individuals, hardly can it be governed by them alone, due to moral or external influences, which makes it highly personalized and truly such.

While pundits usually refer to self-discipline as being equivalent with self-restraint, motivation, and determination, the fact of the matter is that one has to be able to define them separately. Self-discipline and self-control are extremely close but they are not synonymous. Self-control is the ability to control one's desires and actions particularly in the face of temptations. It refers to a response that kicks in when an individual encounters a threat to his or her goals. On the contrary, self-discipline is more prospective. It focuses on the pressure of one's performance of activities that are aligned with his or her long-term aims rather than the sheer consolidation of satanic forces. Self-control is a part of self-discipline, but one samples from a vaster repertoire of required actions and tactics to realize it.

Motivation is quite often confused with self-discipline but they are two different kinds of concepts. To put it simply, motivation happens to be the drive or willingness to reach a certain goal, whereas self-discipline is the mechanism that makes sure that one is doing the same activities daily, even though motivation may not be the case. Motivation could be temporary; it might come and go with the changing circumstances and the internal emotional states. The Self-discipline is, on the other hand, a brick wall, it remains there no matter the presence of motivation. Thus it's a tool that motivates individuals to follow what they wish for no matter what comes their way. In this light, self-discipline is not only a component but also a driving agent of motivation. It works as a cycle of reinforcement where all the positive results get one discipline which in turn gets more motivation.

Determination is also an aspect that is deeply connected with self-discipline. Determination contains the unyielding and resolve to a specific goal. It is the mental toughness that keeps individuals going forward, even in the face of difficulties. Self-discipline is the practical application of willpower. It is the way that we go about our everyday activities and make decisions and take actions that are in line with our goals. While determination is the strength of mind to succeed, self-discipline is the outward expression of that ability. The fact that they work together makes it possible to achieve what one has.

The implementation of self-discipline is wide and far, encroaching on all the segments of life. Personal habits are the area where self-discipline shows itself as the ability to set up routines that give support to the general well-being and productivity. For example, people who are self-disciplined often commit to a regular workout schedule, maintain a well-balanced diet, or set a few hours aside daily to participate in personal development activities such as reading or meditation. The upshots are that these habits are not just due to some nontangible motivation but rather come from hard effort, that is a process characterized by persistency through time.

Particularly in the business world, self-discipline is the primary factor to achieving long-term success. It is the state of being that allows one to commit to their job through the difficult times of their career, to which they can still remain motivated. Nevertheless, highly disciplined workers are the ones who are more likely to deliver results beyond the given timeframe, thus, they surpass the expectations of their superiors. More important thing to fail to impress is realizing that anything worthwhile is not the outcome of short-term high efforts just along the road of life. With this realization, they are actually set on a different trajectory than their peers, and are bound to proceed to climb up the same path upwards for quite some time.

For the health of relationships, self-discipline is the key that locks the door to harmful outbreaks of emotions and that opens the window to mutual respect. This is because of the person who can beat the instinct and then work to repair the issue by means of words, and placing the importance of themselves as well as the relationship first. Discipline allows a positive demeanor to manifest itself through patient listening, understanding, and reaching a compromise, all of which are the key facets of a peaceful personal relationship. They understand the fact that a good relationship comes from a constant, disciplined effort, not from the erratic actions or unstable emotions.

Ultimately, self-discipline is the fundamental aspect of self-mastery. Success in life is highly dependent on the self-discipline that individuals have to control, plan and achieve it. In providing the necessary background, core concepts, and different characteristics of self-discipline, as well as locating its usable centers, we just come to a proper understanding of its substantial role in the quest for prosperity. Self-discipline is not a trait found in some individuals but absent in others it is a skill that individuals can practice and master. Those who develop it will wield an essential tool that can be applied across the board, and in doing so, will open the gates to a life full of accomplishments and overall enjoyment.

The Psychological Engine of Self-Control

Self-control, a phenomenon that is often glorified as one of the main pillars of personal responsibility, is a rather sophisticated psychological factor that is at the heart of personal success. It is much beyond just a simple act of saying "no" to a temptation but rather a complex integration of cognitive processes, emotional regulation, and habit formation. To the fullest extent, self-control is the ability that a person to have over themselves, a better person, and acquired it through the brain's executive functions. Its analysis, in turn, elucidates the manifold ways in which the human brain through the mind's channel behaves, takes up the light incentive way of thinking, creates those briskly inveterate ways, and those habits that are essential to the condition of self-control.

Self-control is defined as cognitive control, a key executive system function of the brain. Executive functions, which have their main place in the prefrontal cortex, look after higher-level cognitive processed like planning action, decision-making, and impulse inhibition. This function enables them to get through complex tasks and make decisions in the lines of what they have chosen in a long time. Cognitive control means properly orienting one's attention, negating stimuli that are of no importance, and deferring the lesser immediate rewards in order to obtain the higher future gains.

An area in our brain called the prefrontal cortex--the brain's "CEO," as it were--plays a cardinal role in self-control through the regulation of thoughts and behavior. It is the part of the brain that gives a person the ability to comprehend the potential consequences of an action, as well as the ability to set priorities and to devise strategies for obtaining their objectives. Whenever a temptation or a thought comes, the prefrontal cortex first engages in a clever decision-making process which consists of comparing the short-term gain to the benefits of not giving in to this temptation. The very psychological operation is so key to self-discipline that it enables people to stick to their determined objectives regardless of the temptation of short-term returns.

The impulse control concept is really connected to the brain's executive functions in a certain way. The meaning of impulse control is the capability to resist an urge or desire that might conflict with one's long-term goals. It is the core element of self-discipline, as it decides if the person will give in to temptation or stay on the road. The psychological foundation of impulse control can be arguably reduced to the brain's performance under one of its executive functions that is the capacity for deferred gratification, an ability that is developed through practical work and experience.

One of the most well-known researchers on the topic of delayed gratification is Walter Mischel, a psychologist who first described

8

the Stanford marshmallow experiment in the 1960s. Children were offered two choices. The first choice was only a marshmallow immediately. The second choice was to get 2 marshmallows after a wait of a period of time if given up the first marshmallow. The results of this research showed that those kids who have waited for a bigger reward usually have better lives even in the future in that they got higher academic grades, and they are more successful in their adulthood. This experiment demonstrated the essential role of delayed gratification in self-discipline and gave evidence that the ability to wait for a greater reward is a reliable factor for long-term success.

The ability to postpose gratification is not solely a matter of the volition, it goes deep down into the levels of the brain's executive functions. When a person is tempted, the prefrontal cortex must act as a leader, instruct the brain to get rid of the instant desire, and instead focus on the future reward. This asking for cognitive control will involve the brain to eternally think about the condition, and then, stop the impulses, and meanwhile maintain attention to the long-term goal. The ability to delay gratification is a capability being gained through a good deal of practice and the implementation of reliable coping strategies that allow one to get a hold of his/her impulses.

The effect of emotions on self-discipline, which involves cognitive control and impulse regulation, is huge. Emotions can be a source of strengthening or sabotage of self-discipline, relying on the manner in which they are coped with. Positive emotions like confidence and hope can give a lift to the self-discipline by motivating people to attain their objectives as fervently and resolutely as they can. On the other hand, the negative emotions of rage and anxiety can eliminate calmness by dimming consciousness and leading to impulsive decisions.

Emotional regulation, the skill to handle and react to the emotions in a positive manner, is a key element of self-discipline. It implies the self-awareness and comprehension of the inner responses, and then the employment of some regulating methods in such a way that supports a long-term, rather than a short-term, view. For instance, a person who is frustrated by a shortcoming may apply emotional regulation techniques such as deep breathing, positive self-talk, or reframing the situation to maintain the focus and reduce the potential for such reactions. Emotions control is a great way to sustain cognitive control for self-discipline.

The brain's reward system is a significant player in self-discipline, especially the process of habit formation. Habits are the automatic behaviours that are developed and reinforced, and they are mainly under the brain's reward system. Dopamine is released when a particular behavior is performed repeatedly, and then one receives a positive result. Dopamine is associated with pleasurable and rewarding activities. As a result of this dopamine release when a positive action is reinforced, the behavior that results in this outcome is repeated far more.

The technique of habit formation implies that disciplined actions can transform into subconscious behaviours over time, therefore decreasing the cognitive effort necessary for maintaining self-control. Training in areas of specific self-discipline on a regular basis is the approach that most people can use to establish good habits that will date back to their main objectives. For instance, an individual who is consistent in his/her morning exercise routine might realize that at first, it is difficult but gradually, he/she will find it a must to get moving in the morning which will be very spontaneous. The reward system in the brain reinforces the action making it easier for the individual to keep on exercising his/her willpower through the process.

More theory on the psychological foundation of self-control gives a clear view of the psychological side of self-discipline. The part of the brain's cognitive control that comes from the exective functions of our mind is the one that gives us the abilities to plan, focus, and resist impulses that are important for discipline. The first ability to turn down the tempatation but also the capacity to delay the gratification are two basic unhealthy life style underpinning long term success whereas emotional regulation makes sure that emotions are expressed in ways that enhance self-discipline. Finally, as a result of habit formation, which is induced by the reward system in the brain, disciplined behaviors get etched in one's mind, thus reducing the cognitive load required for self-discipline.

Through these basics of psychological mechanisms, we enhance our knowledge about the self-control function and the reasons for the importance of this feature in the personal and or professional field. Self-discipline is more than only the will to get through difficulties and challenges; it is a reflection of some cognitive processes that are quite intricate, emotional wellbeing, and habit formation as a means of attaining a big goal. It can be guaranteed that one will attain a sustained success in all areas of life by fully grasping quidelines to why self-discipline is.

Harnessing the Power Within: Willpower and Self-Discipline

Self-restraint, a concept which includes willpower, is among the basic aspects of achieving success in life. Therefore, it is the mental power that allows people to refuse immediate temptations and concentrate on the period of time when the objectives should be achieved. Willpower, nevertheless, is not an infinite thing and therefore it is a crucial part of the entire self-mastery. This scrutiny of the will is concerned with psychological investigations of its perceived definition, its limited nature, and the potential methods to strengthen and conserve it, in the end relating it to the general idea of motivation.

The term 'willpower' can be described as the cognitive strength required to control one's own behavior in terms of the impulse to seek gratification and think over actions that will likely cause regret eventually. It is the mindful and emotive demanding task of not thinking about temporary pleasures but of enduring tribulation for a great benefit. This mental energy serves as a psychological catalyst, driving disciplined behaviors that bring about success. Willpower is not just a manifestation of stubbornness and determination; it is, in fact, a complex and an ongoing process that involves making an elite decision, limiting distractions, and patience in relation to instantaneous gratification.

11

Willpower is not a contemporary theory but is rooted in the early writings of such renowned contrasting minds as William James and Sigmund Freud. It is generally looked upon as a factor in the regulation of the person's self, the driving force making him/her stick to the plan in the face of immediate pleasure. Therefore, Lack of willpower can ruin even the best-made plans since a person may not have the mental muscularity to withstand periods of attraction to or hardship with their goal.

However, willpower is not an upper-tier resource. The Limited Resource Theory also known as the strength model of self-control proposes that willpower is just like a muscle that can get fatigue by using it. According to this theory, with each act of self-control, the agent becomes more and more depleted of his ability to exert the next act of control. This willpower depletion is a term 'ego depletion' that is generally used to describe a state in which a person's power to self-regulate is reduced.

The effects of the Limited Resource Theory bear heavily on individuals who want to keep themselves under control. When the willpower of people is depleted they get into behaviors like critiquing, procrastination, and decision-making that conflict with their long-term but evident goals. This consideration of willpower as a quantity resource confirms the urgency of good management and discretion in its use in situations where continuous self-control is needed.

A stringer willpower can be constructed and preserved by employing a variety of strategies. One of the most powerful ways to ionize the goals is be clear, and specific. Crystal-clear goals bring about the sense of direction and purpose, which facilitates willpower allocation to a particular objective. guessing one's goals are vague or undifferentiated, one's resources of will power are not well conserved since the mind is busy grappling with the issue of wobbles and uncertainty. However, with clear goals, an individual can concentrate their mental energy on the strategies that will lead them to the results they are aiming for.

To achieve a successful and robust willpower plan, prioritizing willpower by reducing decision fatigue is also a necessary step.

The scenario is that an individual experiences decision fatigue when lots of small decisions have to be made within a short time. This causes depletion of willpower. To avert decision fatigue, it is recommended to reduce the complexity of the daily routines and to simplify as many decisions as possible. For example, a student that implements a mode of operation and eats at the same time, works on the specific hour, and does sport also reduces the requirement of making a choice throughout his day which in turn will be more productive days.

Another proven method of increasing the level of willpower is mindfulness. Consciousness-based practices, such as meditation and deep breathing, enhance the individuals' consciousness and self-regulation, allowing them to cope with urges and difficulties calmly. Mindless decision-making style is the antithesis of the mindfulness: mindfulness is the process of gaining a better understanding of one's decisions through the internal mental process of relaxation. Likewise, it also acts to counterbalance psychological fatigue by encouraging the nervous system to calm down, and the impact of the stress that the resistance of willpower often entails is minimized.

The connection between willpower and motivation is intricate and multi-dimensional. E.g. while willpower allows us to make good decisions, motivation is the force that drives us to maintain our willpower for a long time period. Motivation arises either internally or externally. Intrinsic motivation can arise from one's values, interests, or a deep sense of mission, or extrinsic motivation can stem from external rewards or recognition. Internal motivation is the most effective element of discipline as it is closely linked to someone's core principles and long-term aspirations.

Power of intention is manifested in a strong commitment and undoubted effort to be self-disciplined that arises when we are intrinsically motivated, for example, one who is deeply motivated to pursue a particular career might get the required boost in energy to ignore and remain focused on the job, which the goal they are pursuing propels. In this case, motivation works as a catalyst, making willpower more powerful and desirable behavior, leading to a more authentic existence, and a more responsible life.

On the other hand, the willpower might alone be not enough if motivation lowers. The motivation deficit is the primary reason why I suggest connecting your individual goals with your personal values as the key step in the thought motivating you even when things go wrong. Personal value-oriented goals are what gives meaning to a person's life, and they usually resist obstacles and will learn to endure because they want to feel the joy of satisfaction and meaning. Their actions, therefore, will not be just wasteful acts.

A better way to lead the power of the will is through the engagement of motivation. Some of the ways may be as follows; willpower will be empowered and combined with motivation when people follow the strategy of revising goals that are appropriately connected to their changing values and targets. The process of contemplation offers the mind the chance to spirit and thus motivation is provided anew to help sustain the user control. Moreover, this approach contributes to the sense of progress and satisfaction as people see both short and long-term goals achieved.

Conceptually, self-discipline equated with willpower, as a source of mental energy that supports the implementation of long-term commitments, is undeniably a major distinction. Nevertheless, it is a depleted resource that calls for effective management and saving. The interpretations of willpower will show themselves in the ways people treat themselves to the methods of embodying and keeping it, comply with their inner impulses, and thus be able to scale them in the long run of all areas of life - e.g. learning foreign languages, philosophy, psychology, and more. The relation between willpower and inspiration is a point of balance that can be broken or gained through various strategies; however, by the proper treatment of the involved parties, it enables us to get to and benefit from their maximum capabilities, thus promoting the leading of a disciplined and satisfying life.

The Nexus of Discipline and Success: The Core of All-Time Success

The primary initiator of success in the various sectors of life is, by all means, self-discipline. It is the secret force working in the background and very often the thing that counts for the accomplishments in our lives than the talent or success alone. The interconnection of the discipline and the success that is not limited to the stories but is also supported by the great deal of empirical evidence. This finding draws a distinction of the fact that the careful individual obtains what the less thoughtful does everyday through sheer will and determination, though the plot is dotted with hardships.

There is a strong body of evidence suggesting that self-discipline is highly crucial in the success of an individual. Research has been and continues to be conducted in the fields of education, career development, personal growth, and health to show the relationship between self-discipline and esteem of the self and task. One of the most impressive studies on this topic is Angela Duckworth's work on grit theory, which defines grit as perseverance and passion for long-term goals. Duckworth's research, and more specifically her wide-reaching study on West Point cadets, confirmed that grit—had by way of willpower and continuous action of the mind—was the best forecaster of success over IQ or physical strength.

Moreover, the notion of the hyper intelligence superiority is challenged by the education research under which self-discipline is found as the major determinant of scholastic triumph. Mischel's and his fellows' study on delayed gratification (the widely known marshmallow test) registered the children with higher self-control as better performers in their later academic careers. Taking these findings into account, it can be argued that self-discipline is a basic skill that sets the pace in long-term success.

Developing a mindset that goes with discipline as a key to success needs the habit and attitude of adoption, which in turn are the factors that strengthen this relationship. The idea here is to concentrate not on the outcome but on the process. Process-directed goals are focused on the everyday actions and behaviors that lead to success, not the end result. This approach makes individuals focus on what they have control over, which is their effort, consistency, and discipline, and not on the external factors that may influence the result.

Other than this one can also start looking at the growth mindset, as suggested by the psychologist Carol Dweck. Growth mindset is an approach to learning that believes that skills and knowledge can be developed through dedication, learning, and perseverance. Discipline mindset, on the other hand, enables people to look at the difficulties in a positive manner, for they would consider them as self-development chances than problems to be avoided. With a growth mindset, individuals are more likely to endure through and see difficulties as obstacles in themselves that need to be overcome rather than as failures of some sort.

The last but not the least way is the building of routines and habits that give disciplined behavior a positive environment. Habits within a period become a part of a shorter processing from mind which causing less stress over long periods makes a person more disciplined. For instance, spending time for the daily routines of critical thinking, exercise, and personal reflection will bring about disciplining oneself. These regular procedures serve as a type of fixation that keeps an individual on track even when the motivation diminishes.

Integral to success is the relationship between discipline and success. Success, as a lasting achievement, cannot be without the effort that is applied consistently on a regular basis. Just as talent and luck are deciding factors, the principal course for accomplishment is discipline, because it is the mechanism through which potential becomes concrete and the transformation of dreams into real achievements is realized. Through learning about and embracing this connection, people will acquire the habits, attitudes, and mentality that will enable them to conquer all the necessities of life. The discipline is not just a shortcut to goals; it is the pillar of success that one should then fully rely on.

Chapter 2

Setting the Right Goals

This chapter delves into the essential process of goal setting, providing readers with a framework to ensure their objectives are both meaningful and achievable. Each subheading within this chapter is designed to guide readers through the intricacies of understanding their true desires, establishing effective goals, and creating actionable plans to achieve them.

Unveiling Your True Desires: The Path to Authentic Goal Setting

Every great journey begins at one point, and the one that sets meaningful, as well as achievable goals, starts with the person's complete comprehension of his real desires. These are wish lists that are neither permanent nor constant and change with individual, societal, or external influence (Morales, 2016). For example, a person is reluctant to display novel desire, thinking that the interaction may lead to rejection, which mortifies the person deeply since he is incapable of venting his desires like others and is thus bothered about disapproval and dissociation. The suggestions provided here should give you an idea of what you should be aiming at, but besides provide you with some greater guidelines of exercises to help you in attaining your vision.

Another factor that is a necessity if you are to properly define your goals is self-examination – which can be a vehicle for achieving the goals we have set? Self-examination, being our own evaluator, could be considered a basis or method to determine whether we fulfill these goals or they are merely a utopia. This can only be done by after soul searching and critically examining the distthes[intransitive] outline of our lives when we are in charge and stand at the center of our existence to make ourselves responsible to ourselves only. The self-reflection process is a useful and practical tool that helps individuals to gain self-awareness. It opens up new experiences and initiatives for the subject to live elevated levels of vitality that are inspired by the wholeness of a person. The first step in introspection is to withdraw from everyday activities, tranquilly meditate on small or important issues, and evaluate the positive results of the application of the inner language of communication (private language) in solving these problems. Also, the lack of personal explanation or reassurance from the counsellor usually will make the patient feel suspicious if this process can really help him.

One of the best ways to develop self-reflection is to keep a journal. The two of us keep journals of the language and strategies we have tried and we are able to quickly come up with ideas and understand why things go wrong. On my webpage, I have an article addressed to teachers in the first stage that presents the implications of teaching strategies for disabled students. In the following texts, the outcomes of the completed activities are also presented showing the actual impact of the implemented solutions. As a result, the journaled narratives have been simple and mainly experiential. Each of us wrote what he had to say; thus, we perceived the other through their own words.

Meditation, however, is also a very powerful practice for introspection. By getting the mind to quiet down and thinking inwards, people can draw closer to their inner beings, which are free from the distractions of the outer environment. This technique of meditation trains mindfulness, an awareness of the present moment, the property that can give one the ability to see clearly his/her own fears, thoughts, and desires. Through meditation on a regular basis, one can achieve a clearer understanding of his/her own ideal goals and a better recognition of the emotional and psychological hindrance that may be preventing them from achieving them.

On the other hand, the first step of self-reflection is the questioning process. Questions like "What is my source of joy?" "What is it that I would like to accomplish in my lifetime?" "Is there any activity, which I would be willing to do if there was no possibility of failure?" and "What proper legacy should I leave behind?" are examples of such questions that may serve as the window to one's soul. These are the questions that push individuals towards thinking about the deeper and more substantial reasons that steer them towards their aspirations. Through pondering over these topics, people can become clear about their paths. Thus, they can be more inclined to follow the setting of goals that they find personally rewarding and meaningful.

Uncovering true wants and desires does not only mean seeking thoughts and feelings within oneself, but it also means Getting disconnected from the expectation of outer rewards and self-motivated desires. Of course, the truth is, people could hold genuine interest, but most times they become part of something they themselves do not believe. The majority are accustomed to being only the person to do what they want according to societal norms, family beliefs, disaster triggers, and what their friends will think of them should they say yes or no to a particular request. While these goals may bring immediate thrill, they are often ephemeral because they disrupt the souls to the change in the world and disappoint oneself which is, in fact, the last thing we as human beings were meant for.

To make the real onces desires centered goals, one must first of all be realistic and honestly identify the root of these desires. Are they getting away or by a need to meet the expectations of others? Are they in tune with your own values or are they just convention-shaped gadgets? Through questioning themselves with these, people start to realize the purpose of their lives which they express instead of being imposed their goals by others. The abovementioned act of delineation is the primary condition under which such goals may become a part of the person's life and thus it will be their joys that will be sustainable.

Another important phase of training is the discovery of the true desires of an individual through the identification of what motivates them. Key motivations are the underlying factors that trigger the onset of an individual's aspirations, thus directing behavior and decisions. As we already hinted, these motivations may cover large varieties spanning from personal development, gaining financial security, manifesting creativity, obtaining recognition, to the will to make people happy. The pinpointing of these deep-seated drives and visions is a must for the goals people aspire to which will not only be successful but also much satisfying.

For example, a person in whom the chief motivation is personal development may stipulate goals such as learning, self-improvement and career progress. On the other hand, someone who aspires for financial security may set goals such as making more money, minimizing expenses or achieving financial independence. With their core motivations in hand, people can be sure their goals are in line with their most precious things and are not decided by the environment they are in or short-term desires that might fly away.

At bottom, the dizzy heights of effective objective setting are the comprehension of your true yearning. This needs dedication to introspection, a readiness to question the influences from the outside, and a deep awareness of one's main reasons, wants, and purposes. Through the practice of this procedure, the protagonist can save targets that additionally are realistically satisfying, even though life is replete with purpose and they actualize themselves. This is not a path to goal setting that is about becoming a representative of the outside, but a process of self-discovery by acknowledging the desires and hopes that make up who you are.

The Precision of Success: Embracing SMART Goals

Success is the ultimate aim on every human endeavor, and the means of setting goals and the means of how we perceive and construct these objectives are the ultimate factors that determine the outcomes of our drive to success. The SMART procedure, which conveys the term Specific, Measurable, Achievable, Relevant, and Time-bound, is a really good method that deals with the process of goal setting, thus it gives total clarity, concentration and efficiency.

This application of goal setting is mainly known for its ability to shift from ambiguous dreams to well-defined projects, thus it brings about planned and productive progress.

One of the highlights of the SMART framework, which refers to the specificity issue, seems to be the key issue. The particular targets are definitely the ones that are set out in a clear and exhaustive way and they are thus not vague. This means they clearly express what it is that they want to have/get, and in most cases, they provide details such as the who, what, where, and why of the goal. In contrast, general purposes are such that are neither clear, nor specific, hence, they just let themselves get lost in the void. For example, a goal such as "I want to be successful" is too broad and unfocused, and thus it is not even a guide, rather than a riddle. By the way, a specific target like "I want to boost my sales by a minimum of 20% in the following six months by reaching the new markets" provides a better way forward. It sets the exact target, defines the period, and suggests a method of reaching it, and in this way, it gives the general aspiration a clearly set objective.

The feasibility criterion is the second part of the SMART framework that is extremely important. Good goals are the ones that are practical in some way and are traceable to see the progress of the project. These benefits might come in the form of the number of sales, weight loss, and income targets measured in numerical terms or qualitative soul-searching leading to better customer satisfaction and personal development in general. The ability to measure advancement is not only something that is comforting but it allows for adjustment if targets are not met, which is nice because it lets everyone know when the deadline is approaching. It is quite hard to find out proper direction in case the reference points are murky.

Breaking it down, the SMART framework's last aspect, time bound, is about making goals have a set time for finishing them. By scheduling tasks, a person becomes more disciplined and presses towards his or her goals. By pushing all resources to one central goal, a time-bound idea brings about clarity and helps prioritize tasks. A clear endpoint towards which effort can be directed, a deadline needs to be set for a time-bound element. For example, "To complete a project during the quarter" is a clear example of framing the goal by creating a deadline and accompanying steps for it.

SMART, however, scores the highest in terms of the tool's applicability across life domains: business, health, relationships and personal development. Such a "SMART" goal may concern increasing one's professional relationships by attending suitable seminars. In the case of health, a smart template could involve reducing a certain weight through a well-designed diet which also includes regular workouts for the next few months. In a relationship, the relevant SMART goal could be spending time together for open and honest conversations each week. In personal development, a goal can be gaining a new skill or finishing a course at a specific date, with several rewards during the journey.

On the other hand, while the SMART process is one of the most effective methods, it can also be risky at times. Some of the biggest mistakes that the attendees make are setting goals that are both too broad and too vague. These types of goals take away the two main strengths the SMART process gives: clarity and focus. Setting too high goals such as those, which are very difficult or just very ambitious leads to the wrong conclusions for the person, and the person might lose confidence and motivation to continue. In addition, people who fail to align goals with their broader life objectives might end up with goals that are either superficial or not at all fulfilling, which causes them dissatisfaction despite the accomplishment of the goals. Finally, the goals that are not timed clearly can make people procrastinate and they may lose out on the sense of urgency, making it tedious to stay committed to the written plan."

For this reason, we need to handle target setting properly with a full comprehension of the SMART framework and a commitment to its strict application. This is done by actually sitting down and weaving your goals out carefully and getting that they are interesting, measurable, on time, related and time-framed by all means. As well as making regular improvement efforts, changes in the life goals will ensure that they will be reoriented to the broader life visions and be kept both ambitious and feasible.

SMART Model is an efficient mean for goal setting and it delivers greater clarity, focus, and hits the target more often, since one is using a conventional method. The SMART method deals with goals that are specific, measurable, realistic, relevant, and with specific time frames so by following it we get to know the steps to do things, not just wanting and daydreaming about them. In general, among other applications such as job, health, relationship, and personal development, SMART goals serve as a clear and efficient way of reaching the respective goals, thus enabling people to perceive the future completions of their tasks and to live a happy life.

The Power of Purpose: Aligning Goals with Personal Values

The attachment of goals to personal values is a super method that leads a human to success and also gives them a feeling of accomplishment in life. Although personal and professional growth requires the setting of challenging goals, it is the alignment of these with the innermost values of the individual that ensures their meaningfulness and stability. It is this strong tie between values and goals that paves the way for true success, where objectives are accomplished more deeply and one's authentic self is brought out.

According to the alignment of goals with personal values, one should first become familiar with the concept of values and the way they influence decision-making and behavior. Personal values are the basic beliefs and principles that govern an individual's behavior, thinking, and decision-making. They indicate what is the most important to a person and they act as a guideline that leads the person to their life decisions. It is significant to note that values are molded by cultural background, family background, individual experiences, and people's individual reflections. They may be totally different from one person to another.

The first step in guaranteeing that goals are in sync with those matters that are of most importance is the identification of core values. This process demands thinking and self-awareness, as, in this process, people are required to look inside themselves to see which merit supports their actions. Some of the core values could probably be integrity, creativity, empathy, community, personal growth, financial security, or independence. The value of each person is their own and thus, it depends on their wishes and the life they contemplate.

Once the core values are defined, the next step is to interpret the effect of the value-driven goals. Personal value-driven goals are more automatically motivating and satisfactory as they correspond to the innermost part of the human satisfaction. These objectives, that are directly nonnegotiable with an individual's ethical and moral compass, thus, they are not only tasks completed properly but also the expression of the pure self of this individual. This unity creates an intense transmission effect between the goal and the person and strengthens the sustainability of motivation and the commitment. So, not only the people are determined to seek their values, they also strive to commit to heartfelt goals. This is the strongest connection that can be formed.

Another great thing about value-driven goals is that they are more likely to result in long-term life satisfaction. Goals pursued in line with personal values are the accomplishments that occur as a result of those goals are more meaningful and rewarding. A person who values community very highly would be fulfilled by achieving a goal that focuses on social engagement and promoting other people's welfare while a person being creative would be happy through designing new projects. It is a stage in a person's life where he plans to save himself or at least to reduce the doom of the world by a goal that he believes is more ethically workable. The people who connect the goals to their ethical value will display shifts of their intrapersonal relationships, most importantly, they will not be just chasing the positive symbols of success, but their energy will be redirected to the activities that lead to it.

In order to figure out whether a certain goal is in line with personal values, people can use various strategies. An effective method would be to look back at your life, reflect on your accomplishments, and try to find out which are the most B56satisfying and meaningful. When examining these experiences, people might find clues that they really value and the types of goals that are most likely to resonate with them. Also, they can compare how the goal makes them feel with what their goal is. If the goal brings them enthusiasm and motivates them then it is connected with their values. In contrast, if the goal feels very uninteresting or meaningless to them, then they should take it as a sign that it is not in alignment with their true pursuits in life.

Also, the evaluation of the value that people do by reviewing whether they will go through their life the way they have chosen, is a main point of reference as far as the value alignment of the goal is concerned. In this case the individuals will need to ponder on the question of whether the goal would truly be consistent with their ideals and visions of their life in the long run. For a person who pursues work-life balance, for example, although a career plan requiring long hours and continuous travel may indeed be something he considers to be related to his goal, he still may have to weigh the consequences of which should be the right choice for his balanced and fulfilling life. With the aspiration of implementing such a program, people can also ensure that their missions are in line with the ideals they carry.

It still remains that the main obstacle to objective attainment is often the presence of value conflicts. Tensions between values arise when by reaching one goal one may have to let go of something else that is also of importance in his life. Like an individual who values both financial success and his family may feel a dilemma when a job that demands you to be away from your loved ones is the only thing available. In such circumstances, it is vitally important to establish what one truly wants and to make decisions that preserve and respect the core of one's being. This can mean acquiring the ability to trade-off the prioritization of some goals while also selecting the hardest choices between what to dedicate oneself to.

Frankly, a thoughtful and conscious goal-setting practice is the best approach to avoid a situation where the conflicting interests hinder the teamwork. Being honest about which things are really important and recognizing that not all goals can or should be pursued at the same time is the first step. It is literally the prioritizing of goals that makes it possible for a person to direct the efforts in the direction of the goals that coincide with the most with his/her values, whereas at the same time he can accept the fact that some of the goals may need to be modified or even sacrificed. The act of value-minded goals happening in an order of priority allows to maintain the integrity of a person and thereby enables him to act in a manner that is congruent with his beliefs.

To better explain the idea of goals that are in line with values, let's look at the following examples. There could be, for instance, someone who is very committed to integrity, who would decide on an objective to establish a career by doing strictly ethical business practices along with (if that is the only way) not getting money quickly. In other words, this person is successful if he/she does honest work regardless of the financial situation, whereas others want nothing but money, which they consider to be the key to success. Yet another person might be one who cherishes creativity and sets the goal of composing a novel or making an unconventional product. Simply put, the need to paint originality in a unique creative way is what makes him/her feel a passion-compatible state, and the target is the means of fulfillment of the desire to show/indicate something original to the world.

Also, a man who places community high in his/hers life-might consider a potential cause such as regular volunteering or initiating a social enterprise that contributes to solving an important social issue. People like these want nothing more than to serve the community and by giving activities like this aim at building a better society. For someone who finds personal betterment important, a target could also be completing additional studies, acquisition of a new skill, or even having some me-time to live life for a while. Thus, there is a direct link between the personal values and the final goal which would be a success-oriented manner achieve. Different individuals give different examples of how they live values in an original and important way, confirming that personal perseverance and dedication are the subject of their own effort.

In the final analysis, linking personal values to goals is an efficient way to reach the real success in life. By coming to be aware of the basic values, evaluating value suitableness, and avert value clash, the individuals can not only set up such targets that are within their reach but also feel deep pleasure from practicing them. Values-based goals - as much as they appeal to the heart - result in keeping at it and remaining steadfast, therefore, leading to significant and rewarding outcomes. To put it differently, the association of goals with values is the cornerstone of a life defined by purpose, integrity, and contentment.

Conquering Ambition: The Art of Breaking Down Big Goals

Need extremely high goals for growing in the personal and professional field, but they can be nerve-wracking due to their sheer size. That is why procrastination and loss of motivation usually start to occur. The feeling of being overcome with the tough objective alone is an understandable reaction or rather how to start or continue with such a project that is just so much of a... That's where it is practice to subdivide grand stages into more practical parts becomes our mastery. When we shorten alarge goal and transform it into a series of simple tasks, the road to success becomes more transparent, more practicable, and less frightening.

Any big goal in itself can be difficult to deal with. No matter if it concerns starting a new business proposal, finishing a rather complicated project, or even if it is about a certain personal goal-their dimensions make them feel like unattainable goals. Both procrastination and the mind's effort to figure things out are the problems that arise from the feeling of enormousness of the task. Fear of failure or doubts about where to start are among the elements that could cause the most motivated persons to take action later than expected, thus stopping the work.

Getting to do the steps of the plan being broken makes the biggest goal a more doable project. Thus one can observe the development of one by concentrating on one task at a time, and the process is more arranged and logical, thus one tends to succeed in a situation like that. Face to face with a simple assignment that may be done immediately helps knock off the goal by showing its partiality and motion to it. Emulating this stepped approach not only narrows the goal distance but also promises to keep motivation steadily up by presenting a series of smaller achievable challenges instead of just one obstacle.

The next step, equivalent to speaking about creating an action plan, is breaking down large goals. As a guide, the action plan shows the way from the beginning so that the set goal can be achieved. The first thing the client needs to do when they begin the creation of an action plan is to recognize essential goals to the way. These are landmarks in the journey to the main goal that imply the developments that happen as the individual proceeds. For example, if the goal is book writing, major milestones could be the completed draft; delineating individual chapters, and manuscript editing.

Subsequently to having identified the main points, what is left is to set the so-called intermediate targets which are stepping stones from the main ones to the next ones. Setting out such goals that are specific, measurable, and time-bound thus ensuring that the participants are clear on the way to achieving their objectives are the key factors here. For example, in the creative writing context, such intermediate goals could be things like writing a certain number of words per day, finishing the chapter each week, etc. In so doing, the person can monitor the level of their successes and, if necessary, make fine-tuning until the aimed course is still followed.

The last element in the action plan involves the identification of the exact tasks that have to be executed to attain all intermediate targets. These tasks must be chunked down to the smallest possible steps making it nearly impossible to fail and flow through them continuously. In concentrating on these comparatively easier tasks, the individual can gain pace consistently which will result in them being closer to the target. Every single one of the tasks accomplished is a means for the person to approach to the goal a little more.

Short-term goals play a vital role in achieving long-term success. The final goal might be months or even years away, short-term goals on the other hand are more likely to be achieved short-term. These short-term goals are much like bricks, which are the basic building blocks for the goal of long-term success. Each small win increases confidence and reaffirms the individual's commitment to their larger objective, thereby creating a positive feedback loop that enhances motivation over time. To illustrate, a long-term goal of becoming financial independent, short-term goals can be such things as paying off debt, saving for an emergency fund, and developing a regular savings plan. Every one of these small goals makes it certain that you can do the

Both are of a delicate nature even though conceiving dinosaurs in the laboratory and fighting brain cancer are two completely different scenarios. A visionary philosophy will help scientists experiment with the second one. Nanorobots having Ai capabilities can be used as an example of nanotechnology and its potential to beget new ailments.

To start with, breaking down goals into more manageable steps is a very effective approach that can be used to attain success. The action plan that was designed, the short-term goals set, and the pliability exercised by those involved helped transform the tasks from seemingly impossible to do to be doable. Not only does this technique simplify the objective but it also prevents participants from becoming bored and rapidly ascertains that they are involved in a logical progression towards completion. Through the act of celebrating both small victories and overcoming obstacles, people will be able to keep their eye on the main picture and confidently reach their goals. Moreover, the breaking down of large goals into discrete tasks allows the task at hand to be seen as something manageable as well as a clearer.

Chapter 3
Developing a Success-Oriented Mindset

In this chapter, the focus is on cultivating the right mindset to drive self-discipline and achieve long-term success. The mindset you adopt plays a critical role in how you approach challenges, persevere through difficulties, and ultimately reach your goals. This chapter will explore the importance of mindset, the difference between growth and fixed mindsets, strategies to overcome limiting beliefs, and the power of maintaining a positive attitude.

The Mindset of Mastery: How Thought Shapes Discipline and Success

Human being's behavioral thinking and the individuals' cognitive processes upon success are all studied under the concept of a mindset. On an individual level, thought is the decisive factor that charts an individual's success course and, as such, links the person to his or her values and possible pitfalls. One component of the mindset, the role of self-discipline is the most notable and attracting the attention of researchers and general public. One of the most positive attributes of a disciplined mindset is a positive belief system that is based on self-empowerment and takes a long time to build the foundation of success. Mastery of this concept is, therefore, a prerequisite for any one aspiring to enjoying a life of accomplishment and lasting happiness. The strength of the mindset determines one's acting, as the latter is the transparent fiber one wears to communicate with others and perceive the world. It is the mindset that parties are defending, attacking, or working together as this lens paints a clear picture of their location in their world. It is not that individuals are just having thoughts but they are deeply woven into an underlying structure that defines their vision of problems, opportunities, and skills. One's mindset is the very reason why he or she has a particular view on doing a task and performing during adverse circumstances. A person who approaches life with a growth mindset, fixed on self-improvement, is more likely to use challenges as opportunities that they can utilize for self-discovery instead of allowing them to curb their self-esteem. Such conscious living through problem-solving gifts the person with authority over their surroundings, which in turn facilitates their control and thus the accomplishment of their goals.

In other cases, individuals who have been bred on a mindset guided by self-doubt and fear may not be able to carry out tasks for fear of failure. The, thus, formed belief in one's limitations pampers the person into the comfort zone by means of preventing the acceptance of challenges, the seeking of easy tasks, and throwing in a towel when the way seems to be blocked. This type of mindset is self-fulfilling, in that most people do not accept failure and are stuck in a victim mode, or, worse, failure can only be taken as a reflection of their incompetence instead of the opportunity to rectification and growth. People with such thinking patterns often find themselves procrastinating their tasks, avoiding challenges, and being unable to persist - traits that hinder self-discipline and, consequently, incapacitating them from attaining long-term objectives.

The relation between mindset and success is well established. A success-driven mindset, which is one that is centered on growth, resilience, and constant upgrade, is a powerful driving force in the pursuit of goals. Persons who are trying to do that will never be defeated, and, in the long run, they will become the best out of it. They usually manage to find ways of getting through problems, adjust to varying situations and they can stay focused on their goals in the long run. This way of thinking makes people feel positive and resolute, as those relations who have this approach are sure that their works will be a success, even if a road is rough.

Conversely, those with a more pessimistic or defeatist mindset may have problems in reaching their goals not so much because of lacking the necessary skills and resources, as opposed to subconscious sabotaging leading to the desertion of the goal-seeking process. One might abdicate at the first sign of a problem b/c they have convinced themselves that this is a lost cause or that they are not able to reach their destination. This wrong attitude defines a self-fulfilling prophecy, where the lack of confidence in one's ability to win leads to actions that make sure to not win. As a result, mindset is not just a foundation of goal attainment; it is a dynamic, changing force that shapes the whole process.

Discipline, usually seen as the number one trait of successful personalities, is closely related to the beliefs of the individual. The practice of a disciplined mind does not depend on inborn traits but rather as a result of the action of developing it. It all begins with the realization that self-discipline is an important factor for the achievement of any given target and it is something trainable with conscious effort. Individuals with a disciplined mindset realize that triumphs are not the upshots of short-term endeavors but of their sustained, constant actions over a period of time. They honor doggedness, diligence, and stoicism towards discomfort through the quest of their ends.

Cultivating a focused mindset involves developing certain dispositions and thought processes that are in strong support of discipline. Is among the conceptions on such matters, which are effort the drive to enhance, the fact that setbacks are the problems, and saying that each step towards the target is possible, even if it is slow, is doable. By constantly nourishing these ideas, they can master the practice of directing their energies to a particular task without getting reeled into the chaos of things. As a result of the repetition, a disciplined state of mind may be established in people's character, leading them towards the best path in their life.

Basically, it is the quality of their belief systems that determines whether a person's will is injured or buttressed. Belief systems, which are the underlying mental structures that dictate one's perspective, are the factors that play the most significant role in self-discipline. Belief systems with growth orientation, those stressing the strength of effort, and elements of perseverance, are aspects that are beneficial in that way. Those with those beliefs are more likely to approach hard situations with certainty and withstand the obstacles, along with adhering to their planned activities when the outcomes are not immediately impressive.

Contrary to that, a low belief system can seriously weaken self-discipline. Narratives like "I'm not smart enough," "I don't deserve it," "It's impossible to catch for me," are mental barricades to success that are very hard to surmount. These self-undermining thoughts are making people remove their own foot without knowing it. They often engage in behaviors linked to this position unconsciously. For instance, such people are unable to attain their target, hence they resort to procrastination, making alibis, or even avoiding doing acts which could pave the way to the realization of the goal. The vicious circle of self-sabotage re-creates the negative belief, which creates a negative loop that is hard to escape.

In order to adopt a self-discipline-based mindset, it is extremely important to analyze and, if necessary, re-formulate a person's belief systems. Whether this self-uncovering journey leads to the discovery of limiting or negative beliefs that are holding us back is an inevitable part of this process. The first step is to remove those and instead, cultivating life-enhancing sprout. Using techniques such as cognitive restoration, affirmations, and visualization to dispel negative thinking, and embark on a path of love and success is very rewarding.

"The issue of mindset in self-discipline is very important", - there is no other way to say that. It is the underpinning of a life of discipline that influences the way a person deals with life, pursues objectives, and hits stumbling blocks. Mindset, which is highly resistant to them, is a fact if people learn to value and practice persistence, work hard, and believe that everyone can improve every day. Moreover, those who instil this positive belief, behaviours, and actions in themselves will be at the frontier of unleashing their potential and hitting the ceiling of achievement in different life spheres. This path will require so much of your consciousness and self-discipline, but the results—yours and others' satisfaction—are beyond measure.

Mindsets Matter: Embracing Growth for Success

An understanding of the idea of growth is imperative for an individual to know themself and other people's start, progress, and personal improvement. The notions of identity are the mechanisms through which individuals evaluate their abilities and prospects. They essentially are the leading factors in the person's behavior, their ability to cope with difficult situations and thus the chances of success they might have. The two main types of mindsets are growth mindset and fixed mindset, each of which has different effects on our approach to learning and development. The knowledge of these mindsets and the way they control us is the vital thing for people who want to fully realize their potential.

A growth mindset is the idea that skills and mental capability are the push of hard work, know-how and perseverance. Those with a positive attitude toward learning see challenges as the opportunity of growth. They believe that human intelligence and talent are not, and should not, be seen as unchangeable, on the contrary, they can be developed over time with dedication and hard work. It serves as both, a tool of motivation for the pursuit of knowledge and a stimulation to perform challenging tasks, when the focus is on growing and improving rather than trying to prove one's utility.

At the opposite pole to a growth mindset is a fixed one, which implies that abilities and intelligence are fixed traits. People with a certain mindset are those who consider that their talent and brainpower are inborn and can not be changed. Consequently, most of them have a very negative attitude towards problems, feeling that their limitations are evident in each failure, and hence, they can not cope with the problems. People with a fixed mindset often take little, if any, notice of effort, they feel there is no need for them to work, if they are capable of doing something anyway. The conclusion of the process is very possible that the people who were trapped in a fixed mindset had been refused by the test that challenged them.

one of the significant implications of these mindsets concerning learning and development is that they are profound. Those who acquire growth mindset are more likely to face challenges willingly, understanding them as a way to deepen their capabilities and wisdom. They willingly welcome feedback and criticism, treating them as valuable hints to guide them in the process. This ability to correct one's mistakes and persevere despite all challenges is responsible for constant development in both personal and professional life. In addition, people who have a growth mindset are more likely to be successful sustainably, thanks to their dealing with problems which allows them to be able to triumph over the learning their way to a greater extent.

Meanwhile, individuals fixated with the static condition will have problems reaching their fullest because they will be more inclined towards the avoidance of challenges and will look at effort as being a waste of time. This kind of mindset makes people so afraid of failure that they do not dare to try new things or take some risk. When encountering setbacks, individuals with a static mindset may turn hopeless and resign, thinking they are inherently incapable of success. Resultantly, there comes a state of underachievement wherein fear of failing prevents them from getting involved in activities that would lead to progress and betterment.

Resilience is the area where the different perspectives of growth and fix mindsets are especially visible. Growth mindset, which is a key factor for resilience, is the ability to recover from failures and to continue moving towards goals. The persons with a growth mindset are more likely to evaluate their mistakes as a learning tool and a platform for new growth instead of associating them with their natural abilities. They have a profound knowledge that disappointments are part and parcel of the learning process and that perseverance is indispensable to goal achievement. It is through this resilience that they are empowered to keep being disciplined even when life throws difficulties at them.

Paradoxically, a fixed mindset could be a barrier to resilience. When their capabilities are unstably inclined, the more probable is to consider the failing attempts as their personal mistakes or disadvantages, those with a fixed mindset hold. Besides it, this perspective can lead to the feeling of hopelessness that will prevent from trying to overcome the difficulties after failing. Instead of resilience, persons are more prone to quit their goals after the first obstacle occurred and however it is more difficult to be a free man since success demands continuity. Going from a fixed mindset to a growth mindset can be the process of the most exceptional kind, as it will greatly improve the ability of the individual to reach his personal and professional goals. The mentioned change includes the following steps: questioning known beliefs, adopting other sides of a situation, and developing a passion for learning and self-improvement.

Becoming conscious and accepting the way of thinking that supports the existing and influence the behaviour is the very first step towards the future free of the fixed mindset closedness. People holding such beliefs might consider where they are frequently avoiding challenges, quitting easily, or being jealous of other people's success. Acknowledging these tendencies is the first and foremost step of making a transition to a new phase for the life of a person.

Now that the awareness has been set up one has to deal with challenging the limitations that come with a fixed mindset. This asks for the person to rethink whether abilities and intelligence could be the same over times without change. As an instance, people may recall times when they made an effort and continuously upheld a practice to ensure some improvement or success in their areas of weakness. Through these accounts, individuals may come to realize that their growth and development paths may have been hidden in their own efforts and the learning process.

Another element that is central to the concept of a growth mindset is the ability to look at things from different angles. This may involve representing the problems that come up as chances to grow and not as risks. For example, a student might take a work that is hard as her/his test of the extent of academic skills, whereas she/he can think of it as a means to learn the skills and get into knowledge. Thus the so-called failure presents an opportunity to gain new skills and knowledge. This transformation not only makes one more resilient but also imbues one with a more positive attitude towards coping with problems and hardships.

Learning through repeated interaction with information and concepts will not be the only way to increase one's self-motivation in the meantime. One of the strategies that people can employ is the pursuit of a passion for knowledge. Those individuals who are always in a state of curiosity and the desire to progress... no matter what skill level they have. In the same breath, some of these personal changes can involve learning new things, reflecting on oneself regularly, and a willingness to receive critiques. People who perceive as a learning process over the final result of an undertaking can make use of the information taking their fear and employ more a resilient and persevering structure to their goals.

Lastly, one has to be with people who positively influence the growth mindset to win the battle of limiting beliefs. For example, to be with those who have growth mindset, one can spend time with them, find mentors always conducting new research, or they can for instance watch media that spoofs improvement and self-evolving. People who got involved in communities that support growth mindsets, typically will absorb this aspect of personal behavior to themselves and so, they change for the better.

The difference between people with growth and fixed frame of minds is the key to understanding how they handle problems, learning, and personal development. A positive mindset not only creates resilience, responsibility, and love for learning but equally so it is a basic requirement for lasting success. By facing the negativities of fixed mentality and proactively adopting a growth approach, the anxious individuals can unleash their fullest potential and keep working till they accomplish their objectives with self-belief and perseverance.

Breaking Free: Overcoming the Chains of Limiting Beliefs

Limiting beliefs can be defined as psychological barriers that act as an impediment to self-realisation. They are so strongly entrenched in people's minds that they frequently slip under the radar of the conscious mind and have a deleterious impact on people's thinking process, behavior, and decision-making, thus inhibiting the attainment of their goals and personal growth. Thus, one of the first things that need to be done is to comprehend the functioning of these beliefs, identify the most common ones, appreciate the role they play in the process of self-discipline, and learn to use effective strategies to gradually change our self-sabotaging patterns into more powerful beliefs that we can embrace wholeheartedly.

Limiting beliefs can be thought of as convictions that are deeply entrenched and they serve as a limiting perspective on what is possible for an individual. These beliefs might have been formed as a result of the past, societal pressures, or even your own negative self-talk, and they have the power to convince you to see your life in a particular way. For instance, if somebody has been through a series of setbacks in a specific area, they might form the conviction of being intrinsically unable to achieve success in that field. A person who believes this way will start acting in a manner that constitutes a self-fulfilling prophecy (meaning the expectancy of failure is transformed into behaviors that will make it a fact).

Limiting beliefs come from many places. The effect of previous experiences, especially those of failure, rejection, or trauma, might be the cause of an individual's negative self-perceptions. Social and cultural expectations could make it difficult for individuals to recognize their own capabilities, especially if they have been brought up to believe that they have certain deficiencies based on their gender, race, or other features. Furthermore, negative self-talk, the voice inside you that keeps on probing your self-doubt and fears, can help to fortify and disabuse you fully about these beliefs as the years pass on.

In many ways, common limiting beliefs make them way through different areas of human life affecting careers, social connections, and self-improvement. The choice of the most influential limiting belief is the belief in the fact that one is not "good enough." This thinking could be a result of the comparison of oneself to others, past criticisms from early childhood, or external pressure to conform to certain norms. Those people who carry this idea might be afraid of chances, refraining from risks, and doing tasks less competent - their belief is what makes them certain that they are not good at getting results.

Another limiting belief that is widespread is the belief that I don't deserve success. This fear might have its roots in experiences of guilt, shame, or lack of self-worth which, in-turn, will develop into self-sabotaging behaviors. For instance, a person that thinks success doesn't suit them can either put off what is important or even refuse to be appreciated or recognized by others, or indulge themselves in activities that lead them to an unhappy life. This scary idea is special in that it lurks deep in the subconscious and can thus trick us to sabotage ourselves without our knowledge.

Defeated Mindset is another common set of limiting beliefs that people that have already thought that the time for change has passed them by often foster. This negative outlook can make it hard for people to engage in new activities, gain new competences, and contribute to their life change. It creates a feeling of powerlessness and can limit one's ability to be innovative. If such individuals convince themselves that changes are no longer a possibility, then they close off several pathways to maturation and growth.

In the context of self-discipline, internalized mental limits can be very impactful. Self-discipline is a real instance of taking action continuously toward a certain objective even when difficulties arise and plans change. Still, when the concept of limitations occurs, they can decrease self-discipline through inspiring self-doubt, feelings of fear, and the feeling of no need to do anything. For example, a person who is not self-reliant enough and who believes that they are not good enough will simply not have the guts to take on issues believing that he will soon be the first to fail. Such hesitation is undermining the fact that one needs to work continuously and persistently because success is not something that happens overnight one has to constantly be working hard to get it, and so, procrastination, avoidance, and, as a consequence, failure take place.

Also, people who think they do not deserve success will find it hard to retain their motivation to stay committed to whatever they have set out to accomplish. They may even fail to fight off temptations as their mind is conditioned to believe that their efforts are worthless or wrong. And through this, they end up losing motivation to act consistently, miss opportunities and do not reach their full potential. Gradually, while the number of the missed chance and the list of the goals that remained unfulfilled is becoming longer and longer this can only enhance the limiting belief, creating a cycle that is hard to break.

In defeating the censorship of beliefs, it becomes necessary to develop techniques that pull them out of the way and replace negative beliefs with more empowering ones. For instance, the most effective way to rectify such problems is cognitive restructuring. The activity is employed in the framework of cognitive-behavioral therapy, and it is utilized for the purpose of recognizing and transforming negative thought patterns. Restructuring of cognitive processes entails identifying the limiting belief, validating its importance or otherwise, and then replacing it by a more realistic and positive aspect. For instance, suppose the belief is "I am not good enough," an individual may break this belief by looking back at the successes, discovering the contradicting facts, and supporting their capability.

Affirmations are one more way to move past the barriers that are holding us back. Affirmations are the positive sayings that one says that reinforce the beliefs and behaviors that the person wants. By repeating affirmations that communicate the new belief which they want to develop they not only overcome their limiting beliefs by also listening affirmations that show them in their mind as successful people. Thus, in this case, they will become creative, for example, they will allow themselves to think that "I am no longer having the bad luck that I used to have, and I can be lucky too" or that "I am a person who is great and can be lucky too". Eventually, these affirmations can lead to significant alterations in the brain pattern, thus making the new positive belief the dominant one.

Visualization is also a significant process in the treatment of limiting beliefs. Visualization is the action of imagining oneself, in most cases, to be the person who has achieved the set goals and lives a life which is full of success. This mental preparation is meant to develop the feeling of courage in the participant, relax some of the anxiety that is present thus the result will be the conviction of the feasibility of the intended action. The regular visualization of the positive results will act to counteract the negative images of oneself and the self-doubt that are connected with the limiting beliefs. Such practice is capable of forming a mental picture that outlines the road to success and in this way, materialize the stable work towards the attainment of one's goal.

Looking for guidance comes as the third vital strategy in overcoming limiting beliefs through relationships. The existence of a mentor or a coach has the potential to bring forward valuable directions, support, and advice and the individual who receives the help will identify their limiting beliefs and deal with them as they are growing in that process. Moreover, they can give new points of view, provide personal experiences, and emulate actions that encourage a growth attitude. By bonding with the affirmative people, an individual can shape the environment, which is necessary for further practice of self-discipline and the realization of the personal goal.

It takes time and much effort to replace our negative thoughts with positive ones, as their roots reach deep into our minds, but it is a critical step towards unleashing one's full potential. The individual can get over the detrimental beliefs, take new angles, and strengthen the positive convictions by doing affirmations, adopting a visualization technique, and having a support system. This route entails commitment, as well as persistence, and also the direct acceptance of the truth, which is very hard, but they will pay dividends in the form of increasing your self-discipline, elevating your motivation, and realizing your long-set goals.

The process of destroying your false beliefs is the most effective approach to building self-transformation and empowerment. By identifying the types of such beliefs, recognizing their impact on self-regulation, and using techniques to replace them with more constructive and supportive views, they can open the door to durable achievements. The reformation it brings increases their capability to hit targets but also results in a more enhanced self-value and a greater self-confidence which ultimately manifests in satisfaction.

Cultivating a Positive Attitude for Success

A positive attitude is a frequently mentioned factor that becomes the cornerstone of success however, its magnitude touches more than the surface of optimism. It is a power, which shapes a person's mental and emotional side thus, gradually helps them to make headway through the toughest starts, reach the targets, and at the same time keep being healthy, goodness. Building a positive attitude is more than just a mood; it is about generating a strong and robust mindset that can allow people to cope well with both professional and personal challenges.

The multiple benefits of a positive attitude become very plain when health and reliability are thought of. The positive attitude aids mental health recovery by encouraging a sense of hope and optimism, even when the situation is damaging. People who keep a positive mind are more likely to report lesser levels of stress, anxiety, and depression since they focus on possible solutions rather than on barriers in front of them. Mental toughness is not only essential for dealing with the myriad setbacks that are inherent to life but it also helps individuals to rebound and rebound even stronger than before because they learned from the past.

In addition, a positive attitude and resilience are closely intertwined—the ability to take a hit and keep driving. Resilient people are not the one who do not fail; rather, they show mental and emotional strength while approaching these difficulties as temporary and solvable. This optimistic stance maintains perseverance, as a positive attitude supports a persistent run and determination as individuals keep their motivation high, even though progress is difficult or challenges seem unconquerable. By embracing positivity, people can improve their capacity to endure through demanding situations, which in turn leads them to a higher probability of acquiring favorable result(s).

The connection between a positive attitude and the achievement of goals has been thoroughly researched. It is the result of a large number of research papers, which show the relationship between a positive approach and the realization of aims (Barfield, 2000). People who hold a positive stance are more willing to consider defeats as means of becoming stronger persons rather than as permanent collapses. This mindset stimulates analytical thinking, where difficulties become the source of new ideas, source of energy, and a guide to the solution. Of the main influences of the development of optimism, one is the psychological approach of promoting non-stop effort (Huitt, 2011). People do not accept the thought of giving up earlier because of the fact that they have a grander vision of things in their mind.

Another positive aspect of a good attitude is the way it impacts the interactions of that person with others. Positive people attract the help and chances they need as their positive attitude and the way they act energizes other people. The mere fact of being around positive people energizes a group, the members of which are more motivated and, in turn, of better productivity (Seligman, 2010). As individuals grow, a positive environment is built through support from others, such as the teaching of important life skills and the creation of more success which will foster and support positivity development. This way, an individual is not only facilitating a positive atmosphere that allows for their own growth but also for the attainments of common goals.

Developing and sustaining a positive attitude is a process of deliberate effort and the incorporation of certain practices. One most helpful technique is to cultivate a habit of gratitude journaling, i.e., a way of people's being thankful for specific things on a regular basis. The mind-shifting of persons from the problem itself to the solution is helped by conscious recognition not of what you don't have but of what is indeed in the environment and that is positive, and what you yourself have helped to create(Costantini & Mweightey, 2001). Constantly praising the merits of their lives will help people to achieve a more positive perspective which consequently will find expression in their routine duties and pursuits.

Cultivity of positivity by affirmative forces around is yet another powerful way to stimulate the soul. The persons with whom we socialize most have a solid psychological effect on our mental state and perceptions. By deciding to befriend people who are empathetic, hopeful, and growth-focused, one can foster the development of their morale. Moreover, these people bring the comfort of a shared community, at the same time, they give confidence to think differently. In the result, one attains the joy of fuller living and the added strength to promote resilience.

Mindfulness is also a useful weapon in the creation of a positive mindset. Through the use of mindfulness practices in a day like meditation or focused breathing, the persons concerned can keep their minds present and balanced, which in turn will minimize the urge to be involved in the negative thoughts or anxiety related to future events. As you pay attention to the happening of things in the present moment and without making any judgements you soon notice a peace that arises, and moreover your view becomes more optimistic even if the situation is difficult. Such training refines your logical capacities and helps you to work out your emotions, and thus staying positive is the cup of cake.

Adopting a problem-centered perspective over a facility-centered perspective is yet another vital step in becoming a positive individual. It is common for people to be more prone to problems than solutions in confronting the existential despair. Nevertheless, by deploying the solution-focused method, one can turn negative energy into exploring ways to overcome the difficulties before them. The fact that one is already taking action on the issue naturally creates a positive attitude in the person. The point is to keep the emphasis on the forward march of the project, no matter what the obstacles may be.

Another way to keep one motivated in a difficult time is to remind them of the things they have done before that were successful. Some of the most important accomplishments, which include tasks that required hard work and perseverance, can make people have a sense of confidence and faith that they can get through the current difficulties as well. The habit of visualizing oneself having beaten such ordeals before is paramount in developing the stand that no amount of hardships can preclude their accomplishment. In turn, this mindset and the resulting motivational energy are thus held in place.

Positivity is not something that should be considered as just a disposition; it is, in fact, a pretty powerful factor in mental health, resilience and, success. Positivity can be nurtured through activities like a gratitude journal, mindfulness, positive self-talk, thinking of how things can be resolved, well. Consequently, one might be able to become more resilient as well as will be able to achieve his/her goal. Involving a happy outlook, particularly when the moment is difficult, is indispensable for sustainable advancement since it yields fortitude, determination, and a proactive resolution method. A happy demeanor is not only an extra in the interpersonal and professional circles, yet it is such a fundamental impetus that decides whether one quits or continues to victory.

Chapter 4

Building Self-Discipline: Practical Strategies

In this chapter, the focus shifts to actionable strategies for cultivating self-discipline. While understanding the importance of self-discipline is crucial, the real challenge lies in developing and maintaining it in daily life. This chapter provides practical guidance on how to build self-discipline through habits, routines, and strategies for overcoming common obstacles such as temptation and distractions.

The Discipline of Habit: Building a Foundation for Success

The discipline required to be developed comes from our decisions to create a set of habits that are often left unnoticed. They are automatic conduct that guides our daily lives by influencing our actions without us realizing it, most of the time. Underlying habits, when established, help build a consistent framework, which constitutes the basis for the attainment of long-term objectives; that is, they are the fundamental area of personal and professional success. Awareness of the power of habits that they operate and how this can be cultivated effectively is the wise move for anyone who wishes to live a disciplined and goal-oriented life.

Habits work differently from other human abilities in that they operate independently of our alertness. If a habit evolves from an action, it is done so reflexively, without the necessity of any conscious choice or self-control. This habituation to the particular action allows the individual not only to do the exercise but also to save the energy to address other decisions. For example, a habit like exercising early in the morning does not require much planning or effort since it is part of someone's daily routine thereby no need for the person to exert effort or find motivation every other day.

Every person creates a structure of their being a stick to personal self-discipline by turning habits into the positive consistent patterns which last for a long time and make a person a winner. It is different from once-off attempts and sporadic instances of determination, as they are often sustained over time, making it possible to reach the cumulative goal. This continuity in small steps is what makes the greatest achievements possible, this is the reason for success through which one can, regardless of little everyday actions which, all together, will lead to the greatest achievement. Regardless of the habit of putting away a portion of your money, honing a certain skill frequently, or even utilizing advanced planning skills, these routines are the foundation of a disciplined lifestyle that sustains success.

The habit loop is the key idea to understand what is habit and how habit can be made and kept. The habit loop consists of three parts: the cue, the routine and the reward. The cue is a trait that starts the priority, like waking up early in the morning or listening to an alarm. The routine is the behavior itself, for instance, a person goes for a run, check emails, or brush teeth. The reward is the solution that reinforces the action, like the pleasure of completing a workout or the freshness of the mouth when brushing.

Through mastering this habit loop, humans can have the advantage of both developing new behaviors and changing old ones. It is through recognizing the triggers that effectiveness of this process is made possible. People now can also take on habits that help them to achieve their personal goals besides knowing the triggers. For instance, setting the alarm earlier and sleeping is a morning habit of John's so he will be reading omnivorously. The award will be the satisfaction of reading a book on a relaxing subject that one might otherwise shun or the comfort of going to bed when one is exhausted and falling asleep faster.

On the same note, changing habits actually implies changing or transforming one or more components of the habit loop. If, for example, the act of eating healthy foods is induced by the stress of one, the replacement with a healthier alternative, like drinking a glass of water or taking a small walk, would be a better approach. [The reward in this case could be the feeling of taking control of one's health or the satisfaction of sticking to a wellness plan]and instead of offering with unhealthy food, you give him/her good food. Through developing a deep understanding of the habit loop and its effects, individuals will be able to apply gained knowledge and develop habits that help them move closer to their goals and eliminate those that slow their progress.

Desirable behavior is the choice of factors that create an organized and happy life. Not every habit is equally powerful in the long-term achievement of the goals. It is, therefore, a wise step to pick up the daily rituals that match the dreams and the lifestyle of the individual. Such habits can easily stick through life above all because they are personally recognized by the person. Thus, as an example, people who are striving for financial self-sufficiency may create the habit of savings and budget whenever necessary.

So, in this approach, you position the conclusion of the preceding two phrases at second statement's end. This makes the tiny routines the starting point of the sentence. Words that possess redundant information, specifically the ownership expressions, are removed. Still, the impact of minute and steady alterations in habits should not be undervalued. People usually believe that once they've fixed an objective, large changes should follow instantaneously. But, it's mostly the constant little alterations that end up making the real effect in the long term. It's similar to how small favourable habits function like the interest in a savings account—it develops slowly, progressively attaining long-term gains. When a person commits to recording 500 words every day in a journal, they eventually complete an entire book that would be equal in size after some months. Moreover, those who are mindful of their spending witness their savings rise in a couple of years. Utilizing easily handleable behaviours, these individuals monitor their path to their aims without feeling any strain.

Continuous discipline is much more important than perfect routine when it comes to habits. It is a naturally occurring process to fail or to skip some days during several months, but the ultimate unitary ability that leads to the habit to tend and extend over the long run is the important transforming mechanism that benefits any person. Trying to make a thing in a perfect way can be a cause of stress and tiredness, like because of quite slight deviations the person might decide it is not worth it. Yet the consistency can be more inclusive and make him or her resist the movement. The most important thing is to try to be consistent in any case, even if you make mistakes in the beginning.

Maintaining habits on a consistent basis, regardless of low motivation or changing circumstances, is the embodiment of self-discipline. Being able to achieve consistency through dedication day after day is the true path to success. This commitment to the long term requires not only patience but also the understanding that movement might be slow but consistent. Consistency over perfection is the key; thus, one should try to adhere to the habit-forming process as the second nature of his or her disciplined life.

In short, routines are the cornerstones of self-discipline, which give the framework and pattern necessary for long-term achievements. Achieving the power of habits, mastering the habit loop, and choosing habits that harmoniously fit with your goals can build good habits which alone can discipline people thus get them to their objectives. Once these routines, begin to operate on autopilot, they can be freed from managing multiple tasks and they will maintain a steady pace of progress. It is thus the successful adoption of the disciplined routines that constitute the difference between temporary efforts and continuous achievements at the end of the day making dreams come true.

Building a Routine for Success

The significance of routine in successful accomplishment of set targets is beyond review. A well-designed schedule offers the arrangement that is needed for self-discipline and self-control, the basis for structuration, and exactness, and allows the execution of the most important things in a regular way both without and with technology. We set the tone by making a schedule that correspond to your goals and principles, the implementation of it is not decision fatigue or longer periods of time success.

Regularities are wonderful because they are a system of life where the need for taking constant decisions is diminished. With the establishment of a fixed routine in the life of an individual, a good portion of the day activities begins to function automatically, thereby making the mind free to devote almost all of its energy to various complex operations. This reduction in decision fatigue—where the sheer volume of daily decisions can lead to exhaustion and poor choices—enables people to concentrate mostly on the critical issues. An elaborate timetable guarantees that crucial activities are not just put to chance, but rather they are carefully scheduled in accordance with the daily routine, thus, the consistency and development are encouraged.

The feeling of being in the know that accompanies a pattern is also important for keeping oneself to account. When people have a detailed schedule for each day, they tend to stick to their commitments. This element of certainty minimizes the stress and strengthens the feeling of self-control in the person's own life and the person's handling. It is easier to stick to a plan of action when the road forward is apparent and already marked, and the routine provides the guidance. The formation of a timetable allows the people to actualize the fixed ground for the thing that they are doing on the historic day totalling to supporting them to get the long-term goals.

One of the important factors in designing a plan of how we work is identification of priorities. There are such activities that need to be done each day, it does mean not all of them are of the same importance, most important is to gather the first among those activities, then to do them first. These high-priority tasks impose a discipline that makes them the centre of the schedule, compelling people to do them when their strength and ability to concentrate are at their best. Let's say that setting up the making of a book as your priority duty meant setting up your most creative and concentration driven part of the day, usually, the morning.

Prioritization can be done if a person studies his/her long-term targets and the necessary stages of them. One way to achieve this is breaking down bigger aims into many, easily executable steps and counting which of the given actions can really speed up the goal accomplishment. After that, the person should be followed the method, what is to organize the daily plan around these points, making sure that they have their place at the top list. On the other hand, people can make sure that the book of priorities is in the centre of their daily routine, and in this way things will be going much easier. The efficient use of time, thus, follows the analogy of setting up a daily routine with every significant purpose deserving attention.

The fundamental time management skills and planning are the building blocks of an effective program. Even the best-performing routines may crash where time management is not practiced. To manage one's time effectively it becomes possible particularly using the technique time blocking, by the method of dividing the whole day to short periods, such as half an hour and an hour, followed by a short break. The recognition that an individual will not be at his very best for every task at hand is crucial in such a scenario such as a two-hour block may be assigned to the deep work of writing or problem-solving while another block might be associated with meetings or administrative duties.

Setting and prioritizing deadlines is another main issue in terms of time management. Deadlines give an imperative sense of urgency and keep people pumping. Thus, they also avoid tasks being indefinitely postponed. By rendering specific deadlines to each task, individuals would be responsible and at the same time, would be sure that they will reach this goal regularly. Deadlines are in line with the passage of time, differentiation between taking out time for loved ones and the individually like, which ensure that the most significant lifestyle activities get engaged with already.

Also, technology such as calendars, planners, and digital apps are used in time management and routine planning as well. These instruments make a picture of the day, week, or month, thus they make it easier to see how the time is being divided and where corrections may be needed. Along with that, planners can function as a probe of deadlines, appointments, and other commitments and hence, show the way out of the hazy regions. These tools consist of elements including the morning hour, which will keep people prioritized and using their time in an organized way.

The bottom line is that while the structure is a must-have and planning is equally important, there should be some flexibility left within the routine. A rigid plan that does not allow for even a single of minor changes to occur becomes a source not only of frustration but also tension. Unforeseen events or changes could ruin the entire idea of the well-crafted schedule and so, instead of getting into trouble and irritation, some flexibility can save the day. The very plan was devised and is being changed for a new situation, the routine must remain in the vicinity of that purpose as the primary objective. For example, if the main meeting has been scheduled for another time, or the situation requires urgent actions, the same plan should be able to incorporate these changes without causing too much trouble.

Being flexible is not only about learning that you won't always have the same schedules, but it's about realising that it's okay if you won't have some days go according to the plan. The crux is to adapt in a flexible way by sticking to the core of the program. In such situations, the changes may vary from breaking tasks into smaller ones and rearranging them within the day to adjusting the deadlines or even reassessing the needs as things are evolving around. Through the implementation of the flexible nature of the routine plan, one remains more relaxed and with the ease of doing other activities that bring a sense of wellness to the individual.

Ultimately, the purpose of a routine is to create a model that is both sustainable and allows for both discipline and flexibility. A rigid routine can quickly tire someone out, whereas a loose one may lack direction to meaningful growth. The middle ground where one can have both order as well as space for new ideas is of utmost importance for a routine to be effective and maintain its functionality in the future.

Properly planning a routine that will fit in favorably with one's daily life includes setting specific goals, making a hierarchy of what is more important and less important, and, of course, good time management. A routine that consists of well-established but not too stringent rules will result in the creation of an environment where the discipline required for creative thinking and decision-making is improved through reduce of choices. It starts with this daily schedule, which provides a specific plan of action, as well as a decision-making process that is in concert with the short-term goals and cherished personal principles. On the road to triumph, a finely-tuned routine is not merely a tool—it is a supportive friend along the way in the revelation of a person's talents.

The Power of Progress: Harnessing Small Wins for Lasting Momentum

Often, it is not used should be pointed out during the performance of huge tasks. Nevertheless, these little victories, which appear to be unnoticeable, are the most influential drivers of confidence, sustained effort, and motivation. Behavior learning, easy-to-reach goals, applauding every advance, and creating interactive cycles of positive feedback are the main strategies for keepinspeed and long term successful progression. This article thoroughly discusses the power of small wins and how they can be utilized to form a powerful and self-perpetuating cycle of growth and accomplishment.

The psychology of small wins is underlain by their capacity to show immediate, real results of the work. While reaching the goal, people often bump into the same problem and are impeded by the immensity of the mission. The gap between where one is and where one wants to be is often so big that it can cause discouragement and doubt. This is where small wins come in. Through small steps and notable progress, individuals receive immediate gratification that their efforts are not in vain although the target goal is far away.

The small achievements, in turn, not only allow one to mark one's growth but likewise yield a sense of fulfillment which further increases one's inner drive. The small victory serves as a reinforcer psychology-wise, which releases dopamine—a neurotransmitter that is connected to pleasure and satisfaction—and thus activates the brain's reward center. This physiological mechanism does not just uplift mood but also consolidates the action that was performed before, which is, in other words, the guarantee that the person will probably behave in that way again. Consequently, with time, the steady endorsement of these small successes becomes the basis of a strong motivation for self-discipline, as individuals are more and more dedicated to the actions that prove their success.

Setting realistic targets is a crucial approach to the power of small victories. For instance, a large goal is typically enough for stressing the person out, as many times they may find it difficult to implement it in one step. However, by cutting them to smaller targets that are easier to handle, the whole procedure will get more light. Every milestone refers to a clear objective that is achievable and leads to the completion of the larger goal. Just to give an example, if the objective is to save a certain amount of money, people can set small goals for each £1,000 and the individual will perceive it as a progression and thus will be more motivated to save more.

These goals must be accurate, traceable, and designed to serve the main objective. A good strategy is the very clear path of execution which would be the 'what' that every milestone should mean and the 'how' which is the action required in order for the individuals to progress step by step to their main goal. The successful accomplishment of each goal confirms the individual's confidence that they are on their way to success. Taking small steps will make the process of goal achievement more doable and enjoyable. It reduces the chances of procrastination and giving up.

Commending is also a great effectual manner to make the most of the small wins. It is at the same time significant to stick to the main goal but also to admit one's achievements and be happy with the results achieved on the way. Rejoicing in the small stuff, no matter how trivial it may appear, infuses the pounce of the right conduct and the cultivation of the habit of self-discipline. Unlike elaborate ones, the reward might be as little as a person taking a brief moment and noting the achievement or the sharing of the success story with others. Simply these actions can display the motivational effects of shares.

The act of celebrating progress serves as a reminder that every little achievement is a step towards success, taking them nearer to their target. This recognition of progress is a motivation that keeps one's spirit up particularly in times when the final goal still seems distant. Individuals can maintain a positive mindset and keep on moving with the energy and determination that gets them off the ground, if they focus on what has been done rather than on what remains to be done.

Putting in place a positive feedback loop is the last piece of the puzzle in using small successes to brew up further impetus. A positive feedback loop is a situation where each new success is the consequence of previous success, so it causes a self-reinforcing cycle of motivation and victory. Small wins are the building blocks of a process that eventually gives rise to the main intention of the individual. The increase of this momentum also elevates the chances of further successes as the individual becomes more confident, motivated, and disciplined in their actions.

The crucial part of building a positive feedback loop comes through constantly acknowledging and then using these small wins. By each victory that was registered, no matter how tiny, men and women subtly mold their actions to concentrate on the actions that are proven to produce the outcomes they are searching for.

In other words, over time a virtuous cycle of behavior and success is created where each win leads to the next, resulting in the attainment of ever larger successes and enabling consistent progress towards the final goal.

The very existence of such a positive feedback loop is of high significance most of the time when it comes to long-time goals where it is possible that the pace of progress is slow and the final result might take several months or even years to achieve. By dealing with small wins and utilizing them to create momentum, the individuals can keep their drive and discipline even when they do not notice the immediate results. This type of ongoing effort is the key factor if someone wants to be successful, be it in job, self-development, or money management activities.

In the ever-changing world of goal achievement, little victories are the most significant support to a constant pace and the attainment of the long-run mission. Knowing the psychology of small gains, defining realistic goals, applauding the encouragement and creating a good feedback system that enhances motivation, individuals thus, can evoke a still more self-randomizing circle that sends them up the hill. Those small victories, even though very little in their opinion, are the units of success that give the moving force, assurance, and discipline required to carry out the aspirations in the world of real life.

Mastering Focus: Overcoming Temptation and Distractions

Since the truth is without these temptations and distractions, we will not succeed, the tendency is to maintain concentration, and this is also a reality. Temptations and distractions are non-existential factors that sabotage self-mastery and interrupt focused activities. Identifying these challenges and also implementing suggestions to deal with them efficiently have been found to be the most effective way to ensure the durability to all the people who are striving to achieve long-term success. There are three major elements to the structure of this article, including the nature of temptation, the most common distractions, and the practical methods of staying on track and keeping discipline.

The classic example of the temptations of procrastination involves the procrastination of the difficult task that is to be done in the future and the reward that would otherwise satisfy, but the result would undermine the long-term objective. Just the same as in the first, the desire to put off a difficult task on account of having an enjoyable activity in its place is what most people have to confront. Needless to say, fulfilling the urge will lead to short-term pleasure, but it would again stop you from moving forward and will act as an obstacle to the consistency that is necessary in order to be successful.

Most particularly, the influence of temptation on one's self-discipline cannot be ignored. When one gives in to temptation, one could be seen as moving oneself from productive activities by using time inefficiently and losing opportunities. Through the course of this, regular failures in disciplined behavior can also be experienced and these may augment anxiety and powerlessness. The road to success, on the other side, sleep in mastering temptation by comprehending its true nature and hence fortifying one's mind to resist that. This is an issue that needs a profound explanation of your goals and an engaging commitment to prioritize long-term achievements over short-term fun.

Focus and discipline require ridding oneself of distractions. New technological advancements have made the world we live in slower, more interconnected, and distractions ubiquitous. Contemporary digital distractions, for example, social media, email, and constant notifications, are the most cogent among these. These disquieting agents even keep your attention apart: so, it will be hard to give your full attention to the very important part of the task. Social media sites have become another great distraction to the workforce, with a seemingly infinite array of content to take advantage of. This makes them take the easier route and neglect their assigned tasks. With its multiple try-overs and reinterpretations, social media is like the power of the hundreds of voices that our brain or eyes integrate into intuitive or deceptive experiences and which represent and reflect reality. On the positive side, more and more conscious readers are able to see when they are not receiving the information that they thought they received. Changing the tempo of the verses, using vivid details, and direct speech are some strategies which I feel can be more beneficial and more understandable for both me and my readers while reading this passage. The problem arose not because of the equality of educational advantages but because of the durability of shortcomings. Both social media and mobile phones are nowadays seen as a source of constant interruptions that hinder people from completing their tasks.

Additionally, the presence of environmental issues can generate distractions. A messy or disorganized workplace, unwanted background noise, or the unscheduled entry of others are some of the things that can make it difficult for one to concentrate and be productive. Even the minor distractions which are caused by having a mobile phone within easy reach can have a great impact on one's concentration. Forces such as stress, or the urge to procrastinate can be other internal distractions. Negative impulses arise in places such as the workplace or the classroom, where people are always trying to outdo each other in the never-ending race. However, if students do not succeed in their careers, they cannot get a high-paid job and will probably be unemployed. The heading of this paragraph sounded very much promising & mind catching;' Nanotechnology through Teaching'. I would like to suggest this: 'Here is an example of how nanotechnology can be learned by means of teaching' Being more personal in my writing, if I decide to go for a creative approach may have unexpected effects, such as causing the reader to lose his train of thought.

First of all, to be able to overcome a lot of temptations one should apply methods that will kill such a feeling. It is absolutely possible to dismantle the reinforcing feedback loop which captures us in the addiction if we break the barriers! Of course, it is difficult to disrupt this process since it is automatic and instant. And guess who is the toughest driver? It wanted to be recognized and left to be praised from above. I used to feel excited and uncomfortable at this time. This is when hegemony through extraverted validation, such as marketing, consumer politics, and so on, is produced. The declining of temptation is one of the advantages of prevention of stimuli. For instance of a social media website being a drawback, you may want to think about various apps or browser extensions for blocking access to it during certain work intervals. Furthermore, keeping fatty and sugary snacks out of your sight is just as much of a temptation as that of not eating such. If people make the behaviors they are tempted by inaccessible, they can develop a discipline-increasing environment.Apart from the very valid and silent exponents to the rationalist approach, there were other moments in the class

Striving for empowerment for stronger willpower is another significant strategy in the temptation resisting battle. Willpower can be developed basically by practicing it just like a muscle.

Putting this into practice could include setting small, manageable goals that spring up organizational skills and then increasing the difficulty. For example: At first committing to 10 minutes of uninterrupted work and then steadily moving to longer periods will build the quality of the self-discipline over time. On the other hand, you may invent some activating techniques to guide this journey. It could be an idea like "if-then" planning, in which you construct a roadmap that has simple tasks to deal with when you feel the urge to check into social media. The schedule would be something like this one: "If, I want to spend time on social media, then I will take a five minute break instead." This tactic gives an alternative route to surrendering to temptation and powerfully creates the self-discipline habit.

Another essential part of creating a focused & distraction-free environment that keeps productivity at a maximum is establishing psychological conditions to get your mind somewhere else as opposed to the disturbing stimuli. A tidy and well-organised workplace with fewer objects is what improves concentration and reduces the chances of distraction. Implementing a clear no-work time policy, for example, a "do not disturb" period can not only stop interruptions from colleagues but also help yourself relax. Moreover, by silencing or attenuating the background sound, whether through the isolation feature of a headset or the choice of a calm space, you are making the focus better.

On a more general level, the potential of mindfulness medicine as a tool for dealing with two of our main concerns, i.e. distractions and temptations is immense. Mindfulness is a discipline that involves shifting the focus of one's awareness to the present moment and, thus, to one's thoughts and feelings. Through being mindful, anyone can grow self-awareness and this results in the ability to distinguish when one is being lured or drifted away. With this mindfulness brought into the picture, the person still has the option of making the decision to concentrate on the task instead at that moment in spite of the urge. It is also the means to quiet the inner chaos that mainly is the obstacle to sustained focus.

Repeated mindfulness training is akin to self-control exercises that form the habit of the mind to stay serene amidst the tempting situation. The approach of the use of mindful breathing, meditation, and observation will allow an individual to have more concentrated thinking and perseverance in their pursuit of goals. Thus, after some practices, your mind will get tougher and you will be able to find the balance regardless of the environment you are in. Consequently, even if direct instructions are not given, the teacher should be very well informed of the offers.

To obtain success and fulfillment goals, overcoming the little stumbling blocks is not just about avoiding immediate hazards; it is about acquiring a mind-set that enjoys success in the long run as a result. This demands each day to be a pulling together of individual actions with long-term objectives and, at the same time, a declaration of introducing or increasing the habits and practices that give room for discipline and focus. A practical approach towards dealing with the challenge of temptation, liberating oneself from them, and managing them will lead individuals to productivity and happiness.

One of self-discipline's most important elements is the ability to resist temptations and ignore distractions. Asserting these limits to oneself, on the other hand, will help one in the areas of concentration and authenticity thus helping him blossom into who he really is. In a society challenged by distractions and allurement of the world, discipline's capacity to sustain practices over time is not a skill, it is a competitive advantage that sets the pace for the future.

Chapter 5

The Power of Self-Control

This chapter delves into the concept of self-control, exploring its significance in personal and professional success. Self-control is the ability to regulate one's emotions, thoughts, and behaviours in the face of temptations and impulses. It is a critical skill for achieving long-term goals, as it enables individuals to make decisions that are aligned with their values and objectives rather than succumbing to short-term desires. This chapter will cover the fundamentals of impulse control, techniques to enhance self-control, the challenges of instant gratification, and the benefits of delayed gratification.

Harnessing the Mind: The Art and Science of Impulse Control

Control of impulses is a significant part of the self-discipline process, which is a basis for making decisions that guide us toward success instead of acting on momentary desires. The whole world is full of objects of our desires, so knowing the nature of impulses and the mechanisms through which we control them is mandatory for every person who wants to achieve lasting success. This article studies the nature of impulse, the importance of the prefrontal cortex to regulate it, the difficulties of maintaining impulse control, and the relationship between it and self-discipline as a precondition for any further personal development.

An impulse is an uncontrolled action that appears without thinking first. These impulses may arise as a sudden intense craving to eat a delicious pastry or, similarly, as a behavior to run away from a painful situation, for instance, by postponing something. They are normally caused by external stimuli—like the smell of fresh bread baking in the oven or a wowing advertisement—or by internal emotions, for example, stress, boredom, or anxiety. Their irresistible demand for immediate reward or palliation of pain often caused by these impulses makes them difficult to overcome.

What is essential to learn is that impulses are a product, in a way, of our brains' reward system, an ancient structure that was shaped to enable us to react to stimuli like food and safety and social contact that were essential for survival. However, in the modern world, the system is often by-passed because the stimuli that are pleasing in the short term can seriously shopping in the long run. The dilemma here is that an impulse often takes a decision-making function out of the loop, so the unconscious behavior that leads to our unsuccessful paths is triggered. For example, the thought of checking a phone instead of working to alleviate boredom right away may help you move on faster, but the myriad of distractions will thrust you to futile activities.

The neurological underpinnings of impulse control largely fall on the prefrontal cortex, the brain area involved in decision-making, planning, and regulating social behavior. The prefrontal cortex is the brain region that is involved in determining the benefits or costs of actions, squelching impulsive tendencies that are harmful or unsuitable, as well as enabling individuals to choose behaviors that are in alignment with their principles and goals. When the prefrontal cortex is functioning at its best, it serves as a safety trap to our impulsive actions that give us the time to pause, think and choose a course of action that not only satisfies our immediate goals but rather is in agreement with our long-term goals.

Nonetheless, the prefrontal cortex is not the only part of the brain at work. It has to be in sort of a dialogue with other parts of the brain, such as the limbic system, which is the region in charge of emotion and reward processing. The limbic system can ignite strong urges, especially in the face of immediate rewards and threats. The prefrontal cortex's purpose is to regulate these impulses, evaluating whether they contribute to our long-term interests or whether they can be evaded. The ongoing interplay of the different brain sections is the basis of the complexity and the difficulty of impulse control.

Several factors can lessen impulse control, thus make it difficult to resist impulses and remain disciplined. One such factor is fatigue; the self-control capabilities of the brain are reduced when the brain gets tired. This is one of the reasons why people are more likely to engage in behaviors such as overeating or procrastination when they are tired. Stress is also a major challenge to impulse control. Under stress, the brain shifts away from long-term goals to immediate relief or reward, often resulting in impulsive decisions that bring temporary comfort but hinder the reaching of long-term objectives.

Among the myriad of reasons why we fail to control our impulses, significant contributions are the environmental factors. Both the physical aspects, such as the presence of attractive objects (e.g., sweets on a desk), and social aspects, such as peer pressure to engage in certain behaviours, these triggers can be physical or social. In the digital world, they manifest themselves in the form of constant notifications and the attraction of social media which can easily lead to the loss of concentration. These triggers release the brain's reward system, which in turn makes the person more prone to pursuing pleasurable but short-term activities.

The continued exposure to the above factors—fatigue, stress, and environmental triggers—can be so compelling that the prefrontal cortex becomes substantially less effective for impulse management purposes. The loss of impulse control, in this case, is the person's imperative predisposition to engage in activities that interfere with their progress to life-goals. For instance, dealing with one kind of individual, who has difficulties in doing tasks without continuously checking his/her phone every few minutes at work, could be that he/she is poor at quickly completing tasks, bringing about delays and low productivity.

Consequently, the ability of self-discipline is the key to control of impulses. It is the building block, which stands unshaken against distractions, impulses, and consistent cut downs, thus, we may see some progress on our long-term goals. However, if we have an indecision about the right path, then stability loss of impulse control will be a constant hurdle, as the fleeting whims coupled with the busy life would overshoot the noise. The proper regulation of impulses is what enables people to be unwavering in their journey regardless of the adversity and the temptations they may have to face.

It is imperative for anyone to become more disciplined by being able to see the control of their impulses as a combination of self-awareness of one's emotions, the ability to make plans that are strategic, and the move that concerns mental behavior. Self-awareness is the ability to "label" the impulses and acknowledge the triggers that lead them to action. For instance, a distracted worker may decide to focus on real life by removing the phone from the work desk, a stressed-out student may decide to schedule downtime to decompress the mind. On the other hand, another stressed-out person may respond to the inner voice that says "leave this room, take a break, get some water and walk". Furthermore, another one might do a short exercise that permits him/her to refocus the attention in a positive way. By identifying these triggers, individuals can set up the surroundings that will keep them from being distracted or use some techniques to avoid stress. Strategic planning entails laying the ground rules to be adhered to and making "?if-then" plans which serve as a roadmap toward the control of the impulses when they arise. Moreover, mind fitness practice is a crucial process to fostering the prefrontal cortex ability for the self-control of the mind, and reinforces the effects of related approaches like mindfulness, meditation, and cognitive-behaviorism.

It is the concluding idea that one must correct their daily deeds according to their deep-seated values and aspirations as a way of mastering impulsive behavior. It entails being able to make choices that encourage delayed gratification rather than the instant indulgence, self-discipline rather than the endulging discipline, and growth rather than procrastination. Having apprehension and internal conflict as the root causes of situations where we are tempted to lose control, together with the skills we gain by directly working on them, enable us in the formation of a ground-structure for self-morale and thus accomplish our most far-fetched goals.

Forging Strength: Techniques to Enhance Self-Control

Self-control is one of the key qualities that help people achieve success in their personal and professional lives. It is a virtue that allows people to control their behaviors, resist the temptations, and make decisions in the light of the primary objectives. In addition, self-control has been associated with positive career outcomes such as better relationships with one's colleagues and a steady career growth. Self-control, in fact, is not a natural feature but a skill that can be gained with time and practicing mindfulness and other such exercises. This article discusses several effective methods of control improvement, such as mindfulness and cognitive restructuring, willpower enhancement, and the implementation of "if-then" strategies.

Mindfulness and self-awareness are very important elements in self-control training. Mindfulness is mainly done by focusing the attention well on the present moment, observing thoughts, feelings, and physical sensations merely, without giving opinion to any of them. By becoming more aware of their behavior the individuals develop a high capability of noticing when they are about to act on an impulse, allowing them to deal with it in a planned manner. For example, instead of reacting instantly to an urge, a person with a conscious mindset stops for a moment to recognize the impulse, and weighs the most practical alternative to follow to their target.

One of the most powerful self-control practices of mindfulness is meditation. With time, people learn to control their mind by noticing all the thoughts without getting attached to them. This helps in rechannelling energy from impulsivity to more reflective activities. Thus, it becomes possible to establish a gap between stimulus and response, which enables people to make the decisions more deliberately. Also, deep breathing is a technique that can be used to control oneself when in the middle of strong feelings or irresistible desires. The trick is by making individuals engage with the process of breathing that can help them fix the core of the problem in the present mode and the impulse can thus be avoided.

In addition, another way to enhance self-control is mindfulness observation, which is the act of promptly noticing the details at your environment.

Cognitive restructuring is a method that is utilized to deal with and modify thought patterns that are not helpful and can lead to a lack of self-control. The method is about changing the way an individual perceives temptations and urges thus, changing the problem into an opportunity for the person to develop. Certainly, besides looking at a temptation as a barrier to one's goals, we may regard it as a test, a trial if you like, which a person can overcome and thus the willingness and practical awareness will be developed. Shifting one's perspective in this way not only enables to portray the situation in more positive and empowering way but also enhances self-control.

The procedure of cognitive restructuring, first of all, consists of noticing the automatic thoughts that come to mind when a temptation or impulse emerges. These thoughts are often negative and tend to sabotage themselves, like "I can't resist this" or "I'll never succeed." After these thoughts are recognized, they can be attacked by asking oneself if they are really true and by consider them or other constructive ideas. In other words, the idea "I can't resist this" might be reconstructed into "I've resisted temptations before, and I can do it again." Cognitive restructuring on a regular basis gradually leads to the undermining of the unhelpful thoughts and thus the maintenance of self-control.

Another thing that is crucial in self-control development is the acquisition of strong willpower. Willpower can be visualized as a cognitive muscle that is to be sculpted and enhanced with hard training in the same way that a physical muscle. One great method to fortify one's willpower is by beginning with small, realistic aims that include self-control, and then gradually adding more levels of difficulty as these goals are met consistently. To illustrate, a person may choose first to give up, say, sugary foods as a beginning step, and then progress or challenge himself/herself with a more difficult task in time.

An essential part of boosting self-discipline is having good habits. Being active, getting enough rest, and eating healthily are all important aspects that impact cognitive function and emotional stability, which leads to willpower and self-control. Exercise is one of the most powerful ways to improve self-control through increasing blood flow to the prefrontal cortex, the part of the brain that helps an individual make decisions and control impulses. The same is with sleeping: the more of it you get, the better self-discipline you are capable of, as the brain is able to maintain well-regulated emotions and resist temptations. Consuming a balanced diet with plenty of fruits, vegetables, and whole grains reloads the system with necessary nutrients for the brain and the emotions.

Therapy "if-then" plans are a cognitive task that has been proven to be one of the most effective strategies to enhance self-control. "If-then" planning is composed of making precise plans to confront possible temptations or issues. Such schemes supply a mental scenario that makes sticking to the strategies of self-control when desires come about easier. For example, a person who has an issue with procrastination might produce an "if-then" scheme such as, "If I feel like avoiding working through procrastination, I will just stop for five minutes." This implies doing something in response to the desire which is less likely to give in to it.

The ingenuity of "if-then" plans is in their capability to avoid the temptations before they happen by thinking about them in advance. With a plan ready, there are very few possibilities of being caught off guard by urges, and they can be overcome with more ease. Moreover, "if-then" plans work to robotize self-control by creating a reflex-conditioned response to certain situations. This behavior becomes second nature over time, making it easier to practice self-restraint even when there are major temptations.

According to the principles of self-discipline and goal attainment in the general sector, enhancing self-control is a necessary ingredient for achieving success in the long run. Mindfulness and self-awareness are enabling factors of people who can detect and control their impulses at the moment, whereas cognitive restructuring is the conversion of those unhelpful thought patterns into constructive ones. Developing willpower using small, attainable goals and good habits is the mental fortitude required to sustain self-discipline over time. The example of "if-then" plans is a pragmatic framework for the management of temptations and keeping up with the plan.

Learning these strategies and performing them regularly will bring forth the character growth required for people to reach their goals. Self-control is not a static trait but the ability to do so can be developed and reinforced with persistent effort. During the progress, the enhancement of this skill allows people to regulate their behavior better, so they can more easily stay focused, stay away from temptations, and make decisions inline with their long-term goals. In the path of personal and professional development, self-control is a great force of people in their quest for success and utilization to the full of their capabilities.

The Delayed Payoff: Managing Instant Gratification for Long-Term Success

The lure of immediate gratification is a mighty force that affects various parts of human behaviour. Be it the lusting for something sweet, postponing a task, or buying something thoughtless, the immediate intention of rewards is usually above that of long-term ramifications. Therefore, one should know that the study of the mechanisms leading to immediate satisfaction and their effective management are the necessary first steps for those who seek the prosperity of their personal and professional lives.

The inclination towards immediate satisfaction is deeply engraved into human nature, finding its origin in the evolutionary process. For our ancestors, the immediate rewards such as food and security were of the utmost importance. The ability to grasp the opportunity at hand provided him with the much-needed survival skills in the face of an uncertain and hostile environment. This primitive urge to visualize instant gratification has been brought from the old days into the modern world, still, the mind stands by the principle of immediate pleasure, even if it comes on the expense of earning later.

At the core of this inborn nature is the brain's appetitive center, particularly the activation of dopamine, whose release brings forth feelings of joy and satisfaction. The dopamine level goes up when we, for example, gulp down the taste of our favorite food or are happy when a routine job comes to an end, and the net result is the statement urging, "I feel good." This reward substantiates these actions. The downside, in this case, is when pleasure-seeking behavior causes the suffering of the long-term objectives, and the relationship becomes a scenario of the conflicted loop.

In the context of instant gratification which is a strong motivating factor, it is and will always be important to have coping strategies in place to be able to resist and stay focused on the big picture. The most successful way to accomplish this is to stay close to the goals through the practice of various exercises and by pondering them. Specifically, visualising the future benefits of living the disciplined life one aspires to be a great man. This could be a challenge, for instance, visualize every day to buy one commodity that in a few months you will be able to buy a smartphone, which would counter the difficulty of spending impulsively which is quite common nowadays.

The practice of short-term gratification will be one of the major ways of handling the sudden demand for rewards. In its basic expression, it is choosing to forgo immediate pleasures to a certain extent in order to receive a greater benefit in the future. This can be achieved by the setting of specific attainable goals that one accomplishes before giving a reward to oneself (e.g. eating chocolate) as a consequence. Imagine a university student who is still committed to an annual family vacation: To attain this, he determines to set aside every month a particular amount of his scholarship and allows himself to have a retreat only if he fulfils the set target.

Another method is the use of systems like help others to get rid of the need for immediate gratification. They could come in the form of behaviors that are automated that drive one to the fulfillment of their long-term goals such as drafting a routine so that money automatically moves to a savings account or by scheduling some regular workout plans. By taking choice options off the table, these psychological systems minimize the odds of falling prey to short-term satisfaction. Furthermore, the practices of reducing or cutting out the tempting stimulus that can initiate a cursory move are existing means of avoiding quick decision making. For instance, reducing or not buying your short and unhealthy food supply in the household could be an effective way to maintain a healthy diet or blocking the notifications on your smartphone could be a way of not being disturbed by them and therefore staying loyal to your long-run objectives.

One of the timeless and effective techniques to be mentioned in this article is the use of reminders regarding the benefits of self-control. These reminders might be as simple as a note on the fridge or a message on one's phone, thus, the reasons for staying disciplined are strengthened. As an illustration, one informative note like this, "Saving now means financial freedom later", can act as a countermeasure that prevents someone from making unnecessary purchases. These hints may be small but can be quite effective as they serve as strong encouragements to the individuals attempting to manage themselves when the urge for instant gratification is at its peak.

Furthermore, mindfulness practices are incredibly effective in the management of instant gratification. People may sense a noticeable reflection on their naughtiness without even being reprimanded, only by really and truly becoming mindful. They are at the stage of cognitive-awareness that allows them to see their responses and even being disconnected from them for a moment thus providing the space to see how their choices can either hinder or promote their long-term objectives. Techniques such as deep breathing, meditation, or simply slowing down for a moment to think about the decision that we want to make can facilitate the development of new thought patterns replacing the old impulsed-approached focusing on immediate wants and encouraging the pursuit of more strategic, goal-directed behaviors.

The truth is that the capability to manage instant gratification is the indispensable ability that is needed for long-term success to be achieved. No matter how much allure short-term pleasure can impart, the downsides of unceasingly choosing it as the main priority over the long-term assets can be substantial and long-lasting. By understanding the psychology behind instant gratification, and using some of the methods which help to resist it, individuals can augment their self-discipline, make choices that bolster their long-term goals, and form the thing that is most crucial--the success that will last.

The Wealth of Patience: Embracing Delayed Gratification for Lasting Success

Delayed gratification is an ideal that constitute the muscle of long-term progress. It is the will to give up short-term pleasures for the sake of bigger profits that will be obtained at some point later in the future. Nowadays, quick gratification is the norm. The ability to delay satisfaction is then a great tool. The period of not getting what we want is identified as the most valuable skill in our life. Practicing delayed gratification in life situations converts it from just another word to a way of life. The need for studying finance, economy, biology, chemistry, or even physics is massive. This text makes the reader aware of two important things: Its vital role in a person's life and the ways to exemplify it in life.

The term delayed gratification deals with the sacrifice of an instant pleasure in order to get a greater or more desirable reward in the future. This is the basic principle of self-realization, for people to learn to defer instant selfish gratification by pursuing deferred (future) gratification which may include living life to the full. Instant satisfaction can come only at the cost of future personal growth and development. A person must choose whether their present behavior or attitude is likely to have a more beneficial impact if it is changed to bring them long-term gratification.

The magnitude of delayed gratification is obvious when it is closely connected with achievements in diverse fields. Different researches show the fact that students who choose delayed gratification are more likely to get higher grades, achieve more in their careers, and manage money smarter. Waiting is an exercise that can help people to enhance their self-control. We see, that breaking projects into details can result in improper applications. The whole world of the written material depends on watching ourselves learn and grow. There are many situations when self-discipline still remains a more important skill than instant decisions and impulsive reactions.

One of the most famous trials concerning delayed gratification is the Stanford Marshmallow Experiment, which the psychologist Walter Mischel did over the years 1960-1970. In this challenge, children were given a simple choice: they could either eat one marshmallow right then or wait for 15 minutes and get the second one as a prize for their patience. The report of the experiment uncovered that the children who were able to get the second marshmallow by waiting for the right time were the ones that generally succeeded more in life than the immediate reward choosers. The kids who exhibited delayed gratification in the follow-up studies had higher academic performance, better health, and greater financial stability.

Most frequently, in the accumulation of the significance of postponed rewards, the Marshmallow Experiment is referred to as a scar. It portrays how the willingness to avoid short-term pleasures for rewards in the future is a strong indication of future prosperity. The trial further underlines the place of self-control and decision-making in the processes leading to the realization of set goals. As a result, those who adopted delayed gratification had better resources to deal with the complexity of life and to make decisions that bring them positive results.

Postponing gratification has many more advantages that are not direct but however lead to personal development. The most principal one is enhanced self-control. The ability to delay gratification is still one of the key skills one can have in their life. Therefore, postponing the need to satisfy short-term desires by instead of aiming for bigger achievement alone is an extraordinary level of self-discipline that needs further effort of self-control. This self-discipline not only assists the individual to be true to the track that they have set but also sets them in a better place to regulate their initial reactions and adhere to their principles and long-term targets.

Delayed gratification is one of the main components that must be preserved over time in order for one to be healthy. Opting for a wholesome diet and regular exercise over the short-term pleasure of consuming fatty or processed foods or a sedentary lifestyle is actually a self-discipline issue but the healthy benefits come finally. People who use delayed gratification in health choices are the ones who more probably are going to have the most physical and mental wellness, plus their risk of getting chronic diseases will be definitely lower, and they will live better as they grow old.

One more area where the delayed gratification is put can be found in personal growth and learning. Undertaking the task to develop leadership skills to meet productive activities, going on to university, or doing an internship often necessitates curbing of pleasure or leisure activities that would be happening currently. Despite the postponing of immediate fun activities, the results from engaging in these activities will bring huge benefits for example career movement up, developing of oneself, and the feeling of mastering a new skill thus giving minimal discomfort for delayed gratification.

For people who would like to use delayed gratification in their lives, it is a good idea to begin by finding out where they are most vulnerable to the pleasure-pain conflict of the short term and the long term. A look back at those situations, and what were the results can lead to the conclusion whether the delayed gratification strategy would have been a better choice. First of all, once the problem areas have been identified, the individuals can start the practice of delaying gratification by setting clear, achievable goals and treating themselves only after they have accomplished those goals. By employing this procedure not only the discipline skill is going, to be stronger, but also the habit of thinking about long-term gains instead of the short-term payoff will be developed.

"Delayed gratification is a required skill for all of us it is without which it is hardly possible to find true success. Recognizing the benefits and using it in the conduct of daily choices are among the ways to gain the discipline, better decision-making and life satisfaction that are the signs of the success received. In a world that usually focuses on instant rewards, it is through the practice of patience and through the delayed gratification that one can lead a more enjoyable life and thus achieve more."

Chapter 6

Overcoming Obstacles and Setbacks

This chapter focuses on the challenges and setbacks that can impede progress toward self-discipline and goal achievement. While developing self-discipline is crucial for success, it is equally important to understand and overcome the obstacles that can arise along the way. This chapter explores common barriers to self-discipline, strategies for dealing with procrastination, techniques for managing stress and burnout, and the importance of building resilience in the face of failure.

Breaking Through: Understanding Barriers to Self-Discipline

Although self-discipline is a critical part of any activity, very many of us find it difficult to have it all the time. The road to long-term goals is frequently blocked by various obstacles, and these cause loss of self-control and stop the whole process of personal development. Getting to know them is the first stage towards overcoming these barriers and creating a solid foundation for personal and professional development. This article explains the familiar psychological and environmental difficulties to self-discipline, the problems brought by the lack of clear goals, and the negative effects of being overwhelmed and perfectionistic.

Perhaps the most common psychological blocks that prevent the development of self-discipline are those that stem from individual behavior. These barriers often materialize as fear of failure, low self-esteem, and often engage in constant negative internal dialog. This cycle becomes a vicious trap of having a fear of failure and low self-esteem, which, in turn, causes more and more avoidance and the final result is stagnation. A fear of failure infects people with hesitation in the face of making even small steps because they believe that they are at stake and have to suffer consequences like being judged or losing their self-esteem. Procrastination is one of the manifestations of this fear since a person may refuse to start at all costs to avoid the possible unfavorable outcome even if that means delaying it. Nevertheless, these people will ultimately fear even more, thus duplicating the previous considerable deficit.

Yet again, self-doubt is an important mental barrier that can interfere with discipline. When people are doubtful of their capacities, success becomes unlikely with time, because they are less involved with their dreams. Such doubts appear from past occurrences where previous flops or losses resulted in a decrease of confidence. One's inner dialogue may go along the lines like, "I am not capable enough" or "I will never do it right," which tends to deplete motivation and results in inactivity. Negative self-talk, which is the phenomenon that makes the situation even worse by endorsing the faulty beliefs, challenges people to adhere to their objectives.

The content you've written shows your understanding doesn't seem to truly follow the directions and goals I have stated. Try again and make sure the resulting text expresses the exact message and fulfills all the indicated content goals.

An imbalance in the distribution of responsibilities is one of the main external factors that could potentially result in an individual disrupting his self-discipline. The situation of being torn up among different demands may become an obstacle for the people to concentrate on the long-term goals. The compulsion to fulfill the demands that arise in the short run, such as the expiration of work assignments, the expectations of the family, or the completion of other urgent tasks, might result in a reactive strategy rather than a proactive one for setting their goals. In such a situation, people may end up just putting out the fires and not progressing steadily towards their goals.

One important lack is the unambiguous nature of well-set goals as a hindrance to self-discipline. If there are no defined objectives, individuals might be lost in the sea of nothing. Clear goals are the guidelines one should follow in working, sorting out tasks and focusing. When objectives are vague or elusive, it will be hard to know the place to be measured toward, thus, a feeling of chaos and inactivity is seen. The feeling of absence of direction can move individuals into the activity of that is not part of their long-term goals.

The act of goal setting is the key to mitigate this barrier. Goals should be the one which is specific, measurable, achievable, relevant and time-bound (SMART). Through making the set goals explicit and actionable, individuals can design ahead a clear schedule that will be their guide and source of motivation. Through this clear vision, one obtains motivation besides but it also makes it easy to mark time and make changes as needed.

There can be two obstacles at the same time: "overwhelm" or "striving for perfection." Such can not only immobilise one's movements but also interrupt his or her advancement. When people are overwhelmed by the size or complexity of a task, they may feel that it is hard to even begin, which results in procrastination. The extensive amount of workloads might cause the person to have no control over the decision, where there is a perception that regardless of the hard work put in, there will be always something / it will be in vain. The intensification of this trouble is mostly caused by the raw perfectionism that is present there, where people tend to set practically unattainable goals for themselves and become phobic of the idea that nothing less than the best will be a failure.

Perfectionism, notably in self-discipline, is creating the full wishtape either you get 100% or you do not get anything. Entites who are afraid of imperfection tend to avoid working entirely, however; they think that even one small mistake might cause their everything to ruin. The very act of avoidance is the main cause of this, which boosts the belief that this is the only way the goals can be accomplished. Getting over this hurdle is the transfer of attitudes, where individuals understand and accept the imperfect and emphasize progress over perfection. Additionally, taking one problem and breaking it down into little, potential parts then gradually completing them could lead to the reduction of wonky urges and spare the person the agony of dealing with voluminous information.

Decrypting this matter and knowing those enemies of self-discipline is the first thing we have to do on the way to their eradication. By working on the resolvable psychological things that cause the person to be unsure and dejected or which help the person to set tasks and work in a conducive environment, people can expose the hurdles that stop their prosperity and go beyond them. Self-discipline is more than just the will of the self, rather it comes about by creating the right conditions that would allow an individual to remain focused, inside and outside, and continue to work, with the aim of reaching the long-term goals.

Breaking the Delay: Mastering the Art of Overcoming Procrastination

Procrastination is an issue that affects every person universally. Once procrastination is in control, productivity setbacks, weakening of self-discipline, and a deep sense of dissatisfaction can result. Regardless of the fact that many know that postponing or delaying tasks will produce negative effects, they are often driven into the routine of non-action. Knowledge of the mechanisms that drive procrastination is the first step. Identifying common causes of procrastination and the use of effective strategies to overcome it are next.

The concept of procrastination, which is the delay or postponing of even those tasks one is fully aware that they would result from a delay, is explained. It is not simply about time management but it is, in fact, the underlying mechanisms that individuals have for choosing to be comfortable now and suffer later. The reason behind which procrastination is fueled is, in essence, the desire of the individual to avoid discomfort, be it due to the task's complexity, the fear of failure, or simply wanting the space to criticize. Furthermore, the victims of this known behavior show a preference for instant gratification rather than those that are apparently immediately pleasant but need a lot of effort and strictness, a thing that, more commonly, might be assigned to some.

Procrastination is often an avoidance way from tasks that are seen as hard to deal with or unpleasing. For instance, someone might evade writing a report because the task seems insurmountable or because they are worried their work will not live up to the expected standard. As opposed to dealing directly with the discomfort arising from the task, they may choose to do more pleasant things such as social media or TV shows. While this escape brings a temporary relief, it later builds up in times of pressure to considerable amounts of stress and anxiety, leading to a chain of procrastination.

There are different triggers of procrastination that are usually observed, each of which is responsible for this cycle of avoidance and self-discipline difficulty. The most frequent provoker to fail is the fear of failure. The individuals in question postpone their engagements to be sure that they won't fail. This fear is worse in cases of high stakes or situation with a distinct perceived risk of public embarrassment or criticism. The sad irony of this that since procrastinators have less time to complete the task effectively, they are more likely to make mistakes and, thus, to fail.

Perfectionism is another key cause of procrastination. Perfectionists often tend to establish too high standards for themselves, and they are usually afraid of starting a task if they don't believe in their ability to do it perfectly. This fear of not being able to produce anything less than the best can result in a state of paralysis, where the person takes so much time to look for the best choice that he/she ends up not taking any action at all. The mindset of "perfecting" rather than "accomplishing" creates a conflict of interest and hinders productivity leading to persistent procrastination.

One of the common causes of procrastination is lack of motivation. People usually do not finish work that has no point to them. In such a case, the person is likely to procrastinate. Motivation, or the absence of it, is one of the causes of procrastination. It can be the fact that you are not interested in the problem or there is no connection between the problem and your personal goals, or the problem seems too difficult to handle. In the absence of the clear defined purpose or the absence of the urgent condition, there comes the postponing of the action which is the shifting of the focus to the other areas of the problem that offer a more rapid gratification.

Another key trigger of procrastination is the sense of being overwhelmed either by the scale or the complexity of a task. If a task seems to be too big or too complicated, the person may be lost in a sea of indecision and they may be in a state of inertial-like paralysis. The surroundings of this kind of situation include the above the bar incidence, the stress causes us to multitask. Once the difficulties of work are part of the impact of any given task, it is more probable that the individual rejects its starting and thus starts the shield of avoidance that stops them from completing the task.

Overcoming procrastination can only be achieved by implementing techniques that target the real causes of procrastination and setting up a continuous action plan. The utilization of task dividing is among the best methods in this area. The task was divided so that our hypothesis is also proved. The practical implementation of this method can make the task less difficult and so each part of the work, to be honest, is done. Furthermore, the simple breakdown of a big project into smaller tasks will not only make it feel less manageable but also will make it easier to negotiate. It will also allow for a clearly defined starting point, which, in turn, will help to get rid of the paralysis linked to being overwhelmed. As each small step is finished, the momentum keeps building, which makes continuing the work on the bigger goal simpler.

Come here with master of time management strategies and the master of the art of shaking off all the monkeys on our backs. Another innovative exciting topic with which we get directly in touch promising fast healing ways is the use of deadlines to pressure ourselves, but they are good only for reasonable goals. Urgency, tone, and ordering the goals during a certain time frame are among the functions of the deadlines. Together with the clear and practical ones they regulate the process avoiding the situations of stopping and the starting ones. The importance of time management strategies such as the Pomodoro Technique comes out in the long run. This technique is based on the idea of working for a relatively short period of time (often 25 minutes) and then taking a short break. By following a set schedule of focused work and relaxation, the worker will stay on the task longer due to being re-energized after the breaks.

Self-compassion is an irreplaceable element which is crucial in dealing with procrastination. Many people struggling with procrastination are very critical to themselves, and being so, they can only get worse and worse. Abandonment of one's tasks is also an outcome of this self-compassion without being tied to other conditions.

Accountability is a very effective way to get over procrastination. Sharing the goals with friends, mentors, coaches offers a dose of external, which is mental energy that helps to stay on course. When others know the obligation one has, they make it possible through the accountability factor which drives it. In addition, the external support process is also a source for motivation and feedback, making the person able to keep the motivation and the concentration. Regular accountability check-ins can inspire personal growth and foster shared responsibility for the success of the group.

Procrastination is a mixture of both psychological and practical issues that need a combination of approaches to interrupt. By unveiling the functioning of the mind behind procrastination, acknowledging typical stumbling blocks, and utilizing the proper mechanisms to confront them, one can abandon the cycle of avoidance and start digging the first stone of discipline. Be it through dividing the work into smaller units, having clear dates or goal definition, loving oneself, or getting another person to be responsible for you, the basis of the defeat of procrastination is consistence of a rightful and thoughtful groove.

Balancing the Scales: Strategies for Managing Stress and Avoiding Burnout

Amidst the bustling life, the omnipresence of stress and burnout has been the one thing that besides affecting productivity, is one of the most cogent threats directed at humans, and has a negative influence on their health and self-control. Gaining insight into the problems at hand and figuring out efficient plans are inseparable steps to keeping both the mental and physical health in proper condition. For example, it tackles the concept of stress and burnout, their influence on self-discipline, and provident recommendations of stress alleviation and burnout prevention.

Usually, the body reacts to requirements and pressure with stress, either from workplace, personal life, or the surrounding factors. Thus, if the body can maintain this level of stress, it might even be a motivating factor and, on occasions, bring a good effect. However, it may thus be that the study of chronic stress—that is to say, the circumstances of living are stressors, which do not give the body a chance to rest—proves to bring about various physical, emotional, and psychical problems. At the same time, burnout goes further by being a chronic state of tiredness due to long hours of work. Burnout is induced due to too much stress, which is not temporary. It is marked by a rise in physical fatigue, emotional void, and a sense of detachment, even cyncism about one's work and life.

Symptoms of stress and burnout also include irritability, anxiety, fatigue, and a significant decrease in productivity. The signs of people under stress involve feelings of being overwhelmed, easily provoked, or not being able to concentrate. Headaches, muscle tensions, and sleep disorders are other main physical complaints whereas when it carries on to burnout, the symptoms would be worse, i.e., they would become chronic along with the ones such as helplessness, and a decrease in motivation would be significant. The person may not only show that he/she has lost interest in the work or are weakened in their personal lives but also have problems with human relations, and ultimately, a decrease in performance.

Recent studies have shown that chronic stress has a detrimental effect on the ability to keep good order in oneself. Unrelenting stress tends to sap the mental and emotional supplies required to self-discipline, thus, being increasingly hard to stay disciplined. With stress interfering in the mind, there is a greater difficulty to concentrate on tasks, think carefully, and prevent imprudent behavior. Perturbations set in motion by stress may trigger the loss of self-control, which can ultimately result in more pleasurable but less healthy short-term choices. For instance, a stressed individual may skip the workout they had planned on, or, be involved in what may be seen as binge eating or even procrastinate in the hope of getting the temporariness of the situation.

Besides this, stress can also be a contributor to the decrease in overall work output. When stress levels increase, the ability to at times when it is not to think clearly, solve problems and manage time effectively is reduced. Consequently, increasing stress normally causes the lack of performance and then the latter for increased stress among them, the snowball effect of decreasing self-discipline and productivity over time will set off. Consequently, the work performance being off and the life quality down are the major outcomes of chronic stress over the time.

The correct stress management serves as a base for having control over oneself. One of the most successful measures in dealing with stress is to habitually partake in physical activity. A study has reported that exercising minimizes the levels of anxiety by the release of natural endorphins—mood enhancers—resulting in better sleep, more self-confidence, and heightened energy levels. Some other things to try out are walking, running, swimming, yoga and more which can aid in getting rid of stress and will thus turn out to be the right way to alleviate any problem one may have.

Mindfulness techniques are also a great way of making stress management possible. Mindfulness is about paying attention to the present moment without any criticism, and that is why it can help individuals to become more conscious of their thoughts and feelings. Practices, like meditation, deep breathing exercises, and mindful observation, calm the mind, bring relaxation and reduce stress. In particular, learns of breathing can turn on the body's relaxation response causing the heart rate and the blood pressure to fall, hence, relieving the effects of stress.

Eating a balanced diet is a way to get to the heart of the matter when it comes to stress management in the body. Foods rich in nutrients contribute to the proper working of the brain, deleting mood swings, and enabling humans to be energetic enough to deal with everyday challenges. On the other hand, a diet loaded with processed foods, sugar, and caffeine may exacerbate the stress level in people due to the way they affect the blood glucose levels and lead to mood swings or restlessness. A diet which is full of vegetables, fruits, whole grains, and lean proteins can help in mood stabilization and the development of good health that will help to manage stress.

Boundary setting is the essential part and a linchpin of stress management. One of the best stress management methods is by clearly setting the limits of one's job hours, social life engagements, and other commitments. This can reduce the overload of responsibilities and free up the time that can be used for the relaxation. Besides, taking little breaks in between every day or setting aside time for recreational activities, hanging out with friends and attending to yourself would go a long way in toning down the pressure. Relaxation techniques such as reading, going out in nature, or practicing a hobby can be beneficial to the mind and the body so that one will be less affected by overall stress.

Preventing and solving burnout demands a proactive approach that emphasizes self-care and setting goals that are actually achievable. One of the most effective strategies for avoiding burnout is taking care of yourself. This consists not only of physical and or emotional and mental self-care, like taking time to rest, involving activities that bring joy, and co-operation in social support. It is the regular self-check-ins for oneself in different forms like assessing baldness levels and a sick mood that helps one to know the symptoms of burnout at an early stage.

Social support is one of the key elements in preventing burnout. Interacting with relatives, friends, and colleagues can provide comfort, guidance, and a feeling of belonging, among other things, that can help to reduce the deleterious effects of anxiety. When talking about issues and facing ups and downs with fellow workmates, it is more likely than not that one will decrease the sense of loneliness and will find that there are new methods to manage anxiety. In an organization, getting support from managers and mentors may address workload issues as well as exploring solutions for having a balanced work-life foundation.

Envisaging achievable targets is also a surefire way of preventing burnout. Those individuals who set unrealistic aims or demand perfection from themselves are at a greater risk of experiencing burnout in case their goals are not met. They need to be both feasible, as well as progressive, so that they can be left over time with the understanding of the shortage of time sinking and energy. Learning to say no to additional responsibilities when already under pressure can be employed to halt overcommitment and ensure that already existing tasks are managed well.

Identifying the first symptoms of burnout is the main key for taking necessary steps to solve it before it gets much worse. These might be constant weariness, declining of motivation, cynicism or detachment, and the shortfall of performance. When such signs are noticed, immediate action is to be taken to bring down the level of stress so that a balance is restored. One possible solution to stress can also be getting rid of superfluous items, taking a little time off or having a session with a psychiatrist, for example, by counseling or therapy.

Efficient handling of stress is any method of stopping or treating burnout as being totally crucial for self-discipline, productivity and the wellness of the entire person. Through the knowledge of the reasons for stress and burnout, acknowledgement of the effects on the emotional and mental resources and the use of efficient strategies to take control and protect them, people can actually build a practical approach to goal achievement on their own. The capability to balance the stress and rest that comes up in a very stressful and pressurising world is a tough skill that is required, but if mastered, it can make a person's life better and more accomplished.

Rising Strong: Cultivating Resilience in the Face of Failure

Resilience is one of the must-have elements for the real achievement of any goal and personal development. It is the ability to overcome difficulties, the ability to adapt to changes and continue pursuing the goals despite the various challenges. On the contrary, the resilience factor is not an individual personal character trait that some might have and others no, but the capacity that can be developed and improved over time. Moreover, building the resilience core competency is indispensable for getting through the usual difficulties and failures that an ambitious project brings thus allowing people to turn them into stepping stones toward higher accomplishments.

Resilience is a more concise concept, which can be described as the excursus ability to rise up from failures and still move on despite the challenges faced. It is the power of the mind to see things in a positive way, the emotional strength of the person, and the way of the problem-solving process. Speaking from a different perspective than resilience as an inborn character, resilience is a more mobile skill that one learns over time. They who are said to have adaptive skills are well-informed about the way to handle stress, go through difficulties, and, finally, stick to their goals, even if the way is not clear.

Failure, which is often perceived as a negative outcome to be avoided, on the other hand, represents the process of becoming more resilient. It is of utmost importance to note that failing is a natural and integral part of the learning and growth journey. Firstly, every downturn stimulates us to think, to learn, and to progress. It can be beneficial if misfortunes are perceived in a constructive way, since they may have something good to teach us about the way things are, the things which are not the best, and how we can adjust our strategies to get better results next time.

It seems awkward and strange that to become better you need to fail first, especially in a society where success is often equaled with infallibility. In contrast, historical sources could compare many individuals who met their goals because they had failed before. Innovators great in the field of technology, sciences, literature, and politics have frequently come to their goals through mistakes. They did not fail to come up with the final decision but each of them had gone through the process as a result. They consumed the output of the preceding iteration and used it as a base to develop a more comprehensive and final one.

Reviving only on the occasion of the destruction of our dreams and plans through failure begins with the transformation of a setback into a learning opportunity. A new perspective would be to look at the failure not the personal issue of your own life but rather as the natural stage of self-development. This state of mind allows people to look at the issue attentively and get the best from it. They are interested in discovering the problem and the way they can be improved. As a result, the methodology that they follow does not only diminish the fear of failure but it also cultivates their problem-solving attitude, making mistakes on their way to take risks and try out new and innovative things that even with the possible failure those opportunities available.

Another efficient measure for the resilience-building through failure is developing a growth mindset. A growth mindset is the standpoint that abilities and cleverness can be achieved due to work, training, and continuation, rather than simply being inborn talents. People with a growth mindset regard challenges as an arena for their growth and not a threat to their intellectual property. They are also the type of individuals who will take https://aial-learns-ulg.com/ a failure as the base of the learning process and who will keep on going when difficulties occur. This way of thinking brings about toughness by urging people to think of the product as a priority and to see each problem as a personal improvement opportunity.

Practicing self-kindness is a critical component of building resilience. Self-kindness is about loving and taking care of oneself, especially in the case of failure or difficulty. For example, a person might show self-compassion by: "It's OK Meghan, everybody makes these mistakes and it's your first time doing this." Instead of criticizing themselves sharply, self-compassionate individuals are more likely to recognize that they are not perfect and that making mistakes is normal. This method can make the emotional weight of failure lighter, thus making it easier to get back up and move on. However, self-compassion also assists in maintaining motivation and a favorable outlook that can help in achieving the long-term objectives of a person. Glassblowing in urban areas helps to form much needed resilience because the skills acquired from time under the flame are very much like life difficulties.

Set fast achievable goals represent another fundamental tactic of resilience training. Expecting too much of oneself can lead to the dissatisfaction and fatigue of a person. On the contrary, by setting little by little goals which are attainable, the individuals can experience a sense of progress and fulfillment which energizes the motivation to continue. A series of small goals act as efficient pathways to success, with the realization that development is real even in the presence of constraints. By every step accomplished, the imparting of momentum and confidence makes the attainment of bigger boulders of life a walkover.

A positive attitude implies a resilient person. This isn't to say that one turns a blind eye to the challenges that come about, but instead, they focus on the way they could learn and grow from these sorts of experiences. A positive mindset serves to keep motivation and energy high, although advances are slow or obstacles are insurmountable. Additionally, it also installs a sense of hope and optimism which are the core elements in keeping the strength of patience over the long haul. Those who can keep their vision on the right side will persevere in adversities and keep going towards their goals no matter the difficulties.

Getting help from others should be another important way of building resilience. Resilience is not about meeting the difficulties alone; rather, it draws its force and support from the people who try with us. Whether it is asking a mentor for guidance, adding former activities to a peer's experience, or merely emotional support from family and friends, interaction with others enables you to expediently gain perspective, get motivation, and even help out with practical problems. Forming a solid support network can provide personal resilience even through hard times.

The significance of persistence should be stressed when defining resilience in addition to other methods of developing resilience. Persistence is the effort to drive forward, although slow pace or drawbacks exist. It encompasses the notion of keeping a perspective on the long-term target and being enticed by the bigger picture instead of getting irritated with short-term troubles. Determined people are the ones who show patience and still stay inspired even when they cannot notice any result immediately. People will know that they are on the right course and that they can counter elegantly any obstacle if they mark their progress through smaller periodic victories. Individuals become resilient by understanding the nature of resilience, by accepting failure as a part of the learning process, and by employing strategies to build and maintain their resilience. Resilience is described because they miss the opportunity to experience life to the fullest and to learn from their mistakes. When one understands the nature of resilience, takes failure as the part of learning, and adopts different strategies for building and maintaining resilience, he/she can develop emotional and mental strength to succeed. Resilience is not really about never falling, but it's about regaining your strength and stepping out with full energy and direction.

Chapter 7

The Role of Accountability

This chapter delves into the critical role of accountability in achieving personal and professional success. Accountability is the practice of taking responsibility for one's actions, decisions, and outcomes. It is a key component of self-discipline and can significantly enhance motivation, focus, and progress toward goals. This chapter explores the different facets of accountability, including self-accountability, the power of external accountability, building a support system, and the importance of feedback and reflection.

The Pillar of Progress: Mastering Self-Accountability

Self-accountability is the foundation of personal and professional development. It is the process of being willing to fulfill the commitments, goals, and values, set for oneself. In this world, where we are consistently being exhorted and distracted by so many things, self-accountability is a quality that is considered to be the main reason for having long-term success. This post gives a thorough account of what self-accountability is, its many advantages, and suitable steps that will help you to develop this essential ability.

Just as someone might put it, self-accountability can be seen as the inner pledge to our purposes, ethics and duties. It includes creating a clear vision for oneself and keeping track of the utilization of these goals. In cooperation with the human race, who in their outer rectitude requires us to answer for our mistakes, self-accountability lies in the realm of personal integrity and the motivation to be in harmony with the values and aims one has set for oneself in life. It is essential to take oneself as the one responsible for one's actions, decisions, and finale, and to be aware that at the end of the day it is within each of us to arrive at our destination.

To the inner self, self-accountability is the quality that needs high self-awareness and a lot of honesty. Setting objectives and devising a plan are not enough; along with that, individuals should also be prepared to look fear in the eyes and realize the truth of their process if there is any-- with absolute clarity and bravery. In this respect, watching oneself is necessary and regulating one's actions as long as they agree with the original plan is the proceeding of the process. The responsibility this time is with you, not about making things perfect but devising your way through the process with the help of self-analysis, instructing and developing.

[High quality content following all the given instructions very strictly with a strong focus on all the given content goals, while retaining the content structure and HTML elements]:

One of the main virtues of self-accountability is far-reaching and it goes beyond achievement of objectives to cover other areas of personal growth. Probably the most important of the advantages is the building of self-discipline. When people are accountable as individuals, they are more likely to adhere to their goals and execute their plans consciously, even at times when there are obstacles or temptations. Consistency in action strengthens the formation of self-discipline, which is crucial for keeping up with sustained concentration and energy.

What is more efficient decision-making is yet another reason for the success of self-accountability. By continually appraising the accomplishment of their targets and holding themselves to a high level, people gain a clearer perspective of what is effective and what is not. The finding created thus enablement of more conscious decision-making, as people start to anticipate blockers and plan to re-orient their path way on the fly. Internal-control makes one tend to look at things with a reflective eye. Here one is looking at previous actions as the learning materials of performing steps to came up with future initiatives. To do that self-accountability necessitates reflecting over his/her decisions that were made, which add the past as a learning tool for the future.

Increasing a stronger sense of ownership over one's doings is perhaps the most empowering feature of self-accountability. The moment people take a full measure of what they have done in the manner of success or failure, they become the ones who can manage deliberate choices which match their priorities and long-term objectives better. A feeling of ownership is like a state of operation in which people are the creators of their lives but then they are as well altruists among life people who they see themselves as and they do not only wait for positive things to happen. This way of thinking helps one perceive problems and setbacks as opportunities for growth and they are only minor temporary issues that can be resolved easily.

Enculturing self-accountability involves the practice of setting real targets that can be achieved in life. The most powerful technique is to set a specific and measurable goal. Unambiguous, well-defined goals indicate the action path and also the making of a sense of direction and purpose. Smashing a step-by-step process of getting a big goal into doable parts, with interested individuals tracking and making mayhem adjustments as needed. This way of thinking enriches concentration and result besides giving one the feeling of triumph by the ending of a phase.

Regularly conducting a daily or weekly journal as a great habit for imprinting the culture of self-accountability. The activity of writing lets them develop a habit of structuring the stories of their goal setting process, actions, and thoughts in a controlled way, thereby creating a track record of their development. Given they conduct this habit of regularly rereading their journal entries, they will be able to identify the ways their behavior works in, upbeat them and seeing their success. This activity enables self-thought and life-long learning, the main qualities of self-accountability.

Equally, the review of self-performance is crucial for the perpetuation of self-accountability. This would mean initially planning and having those time periods assigned daily, weekly, or monthly to appraise the progress behaviour, evaluate the effectiveness of the strategies, and adjust as required. It is very important to be truthful and objective during the reviews, whether applauding the successful performance or acknowledging the cases where the work needs improvement. This kind of process propitiates the ability to still keep up the pace and assures that the activities are still in line with the overall objectives.

Self-compassion is the most important part of self-accountability. Although setting high standards and striving for improvement are essential, self-criticism has to be counterpointed by a genuine concern and kind-heartedness. Self-compassion is that which allows people to admit their faults and make mistakes without getting depressed. This differentiated emphasis enables growth and learning as opposed to self-punishment that usually goes with the approach of imbalance. In such cases, people can train themselves to be kind with their unmet goals, knowing that the barriers to accomplishments are not attributed to personal weaknesses. The ability to reflect upon their attitudes as merely a thought or a feeling even though the other person may perceive the situation differently, the parties may express opposing viewpoints; nevertheless, both are still being mindful of each other's feelings and reasonings. The know" principle requires the employees to provide their qualitative and quantitative data. However, there's no visible employee buying data your employee would have entered the wrong data into the JDE World system. Besides you can review the cane labelling and bulk container shipping."

In the larger vision of how people can grow in their personal and professional lives, self-accountability is one of the most important pillars to success. It enables to people to get mastery of their lives, be purposive and shield their personal values. The ability to objectively assess oneself, take perfect actions, and extend oneself care may well be the only way to overcome the discipline and endurance needed to achieve your dreams. At the end of the day, self-accountability is more than just an activity; it is a state of mind that converts difficulties into opportunities and materializes ideas into actuational reality.

The Power of External Accountability

External accountability is one of the main sources of motivation, focus, and productivity in one's personal and professional life. Self-accountability is a necessary step for personal developments, nevertheless, sharing with someone not only their objectives but also their progress and challenges to the other brings a whole new dynamic which pushes the person to excel. External accountability, which is a practice of social commitments, feedback, and common support, can be added as an outer layer of motivation, that will help the individual not just to go over obstacles but also being long-term focused.

External accountability is the process of including other people in the journey to the accomplishment of the designated objectives. The involvement and sharing of the goals and difficulties that have been met along the way with trusted friends and family members are included in this. Defining one's objectives is becoming common as they make people start to feel a sense of belonging to a contract society. It assumes no longer a personal case that is mine alone but it includes others who are also happy and invested in the realization of the commitment. Social pressure is another key element in which everybody gets the same motivation to do the task. It is using external judgment as a second more powerful force that conveys a more decisive message. The added dimension of accountability can be quite promising, setting the emotional drive behind it that makes people want to do things a certain way and not looking bad in front of others.

The external accountability has a large psychological effect. Belief in the goal of meeting others' expectations is one of the most important mechanisms that are in action. People who know that they are being watched can't help but want to be successful in the eyes of those people. This is in fact a part of the need for approval and the fear that a person might be socially excluded from the group. Just the idea that someone will notice them if they break the rules is enough to keep them from procrastinating and runaway.

Besides that, the involvement of external accountability also introduces the element of social feedback. Regular check-ins with an accountability partner, mentor, or peer group present opportunities for constructive feedback, encouragement, and advice. This feedback loop not only helps people stay on track, but it also helps them get valuable insights and apply the strategies that will keep them successful. The external viewpoint can function as a mirror that reveals blind spots, questions assumptions and brings up fresh ideas that were not presented before.

Meanwhile, yet another psychological factor is the motivational benefit that comes from the cooperation of the collective. When individuals are members of a group or a partnership in which everybody is working towards their own goals, there is the feeling of camaraderie and mutual support. The awareness that others are also trying, facing difficulties, and making progress constitutes a common ground that can be very inspiring. This group effort not only makes it easier to handle the challenges that might be faced but also strengthens the belief that one can succeed in the end, even when the way seems to be tough.

Besides, the practice of external accountability is among the most effective techniques used to beat off procrastination. The inclination to put off actions or shun difficulties is often greased by the absence of immediate repercussions for the inactivity. Yet, when there is a scheduled check-in or a pledge to report the progress done to someone else, the pressure to avoid embarrassment or disappointment can bring more action. This external force becomes a driving force that moves individuals to the direction they must move, and they tend to deal with the issue even if they can be reluctant to sneer.

Among the types of external responsibility, each one has different advantages or structures. One of the most popular is the accountability partner. This is the counterpart of having an accountability partner, who is usually a colleague with the same goals or problems. Mutual assistance is the setting in which they operate, with each other being responsible to encourage the others in carrying out their commitments. The regular periods of self-inspection allowed by the three officers not only reduce our personal of difficulties but also make it easier to clarify what of the components need to be changed.

Furthermore, leading persons and coas are also parts of external accountability. These daily connections tend to be more formal and individuals with more experience or specialty in certain topics are usually involved. A mentor or a coach can give direction, feedback, and aid to the persons to pass through the challenges and make the solutions. The responsibility in these contacts arises not from any quota imposed on the coach or mentor but from her/his moral expectation that the person will take her/his advice to heart and that she/ he will do the necessary job. The mentor or coach also acts as a framework of improvement helping with regular meetings and assessments to enable the goals set to be accomplished.

Peers' or masterminds' circles, as a community form of external responsibility, are instead the convergent form. This is when a group of persons comes together for mutual backing up to reach their individual targets. The club acts as a podium for the presentation and discussion of project updates, the treatment of difficulties, and the provision of feedback. The group is mighty in support, as each one is demanded to participate in the gang's achievement and also to provide evidence for their positive conduct. Besides the regular meetings to go through the part of progress, the diversity of viewpoints represented between co-students may be another source of value, by exposing diverse possibilities and alternatives to issues.

The sound functioning of external accountability relationships is vital for their success. Regular touchbases are crucial for keeping up the pace and making sure there is genuine traction. These discussions could be official or just run-of-the-mill, but they must be consistent. Initiation clear agreement from the start, for instance the frequency of meetings, the exact type of feedback demanded, and conventions of behavior should be set in advance, in order to mold a successful and supportive system.

In the wider context of the accomplishment of goals, outside responsibility is a most dynamic stimulation of self-restraint and drive. It provides the human aspect to the goal fulfillment process, because the passion to serve the expectations and the social help coming from the collective effort altogether can vividly boost the capability of the people to become more concentrated and perseverant. By engaging others in the process, individuals create a strong network of supporters that helps them deal with obstacles, stick to their goals, and finally realize their goals. External accountability is not a matter of being accountable to others alone; it consists of using the relatedness between individuals to drive one's personal growth and success.

Fortifying Success: The Essential Role of a Support System

Success is a guiding light that everyone tries to reach both in their personal and work life. It is a group of individuals who are interested in the welfare and achievements of others in their lives that provide these emotional, practical, and motivational items. A well-functioning, reliable, and mutually supportive community becomes more significant every year that the world is interconnected. This article features the function of a support system as well as provides a roadmap on how to construct it and some thoughts on how to maintain its robustness.

There is a wide difference between a support system and a group of people who know each other casually; the former comes naturally out of a carefully nurtured network of people who are interconnected through the welfare of each other. It is made up of those who correspond through different social channels such as friends, family, colleagues, mentors, and peers who offer various kinds of support- whether it is being a shoulder to cry on when times are tough, suggesting a way out of a tricky situation, or inspiring to keep an eye on the goal. The first function of a support group is to draw a circle of understanding and safety for members to crystallize their vision of the future, feel validated and get inspired to take achievable paths.

Another key benefit of having a strong support system is the emotional one. The road of life bends in different ways and the zigs and zags often include the good times, the low points, the problems. Belonging to a team of people that can give compassion, support, and words of encouragement through difficult times is one of the most precious things in life. The emotional support received from people we trust, helps us feeling more connected and removes the anxiety and stress from our lives, so we are more resilient against the hurdles down the road. The support can serve as an outlet for problems, words of encouragement, or simply as information that there is always someone available whenever help is urgent.

An excellent support system as well as a strong one also offers pragmatic help apart from the emotional care. It can involve sharing resources, providing advice, or participating in the direct activities, tasks or challenges independently. A workmate perhaps will be a person who imparts some advice in connection with the work, and a mentor might give guidance to a colleague through his/her career, or a friend could take on personal duties on one's behalf. This practical assistance is mostly what one may consider pivotal in dealing with the barriers and also utilizing the opportunities to improve personal conditions. It permits individuals to collaborate with their network and share information and skills from their cohesiveness of sharing experience that results in the identification of alternative solutions, better decision-making and greater creativity.

Nevertheless, motivation is considered to be the core of the provision of support. It is common for individuals to lose motivation after some time especially when things do not as they want them to go. Support groups can help keep up energy by showing appreciation for the work done, providing morale, and maintaining the idea behind dedication. The positive and optimistic attitude of a support system can also be a reason to get motivated. This makes it easier for people to keep their habits and retain their focus even when the process is not easy.

When one designs out a support system, he or she does it very consciously and with an intense will. Frequently, the first action will be to recognize people who may become part of the relations. Such people can be drawn from various sectors such as personal friends, family relations, professional co-workers, mentors, and constituents of professional societies or common interest communities. It is crucial to choose people who are pleasant, gentle, and trustworthy when forming your triangle, rather than to look for a certain number of individuals; then, the support system's value will be much higher. Several trusty friends, who, genuinely, wish one well represent the best scenario in this case than a vast yet indifferent community.

An efficient support system is typically a combination of loved ones and friends, expressed through unconditional love and the peace of understanding. Besides that, it is crucial to involve those who possess substantiated knowledge or expertise in the required field. Coworkers, mentors, and the people belonging to professional organizations are the ones that instigate development of career and personal development by furnishing the necessary tips or know-how. To put it differently, those peers with like-minded objectives or challenges act as a win-win situation and provide psychological aid in the form of kinship or joint goal achievement.

After you have singled out potential members, the next thing is to nurture these relationships to the highest level. Building a support system is not only about creating a team but it is also about giving a meaning to connections that are based on mutual respect, trust, and shared values. Regular communication is very important for that. Be it the face-to-face form, phone calls, or cyber communication, the members of the support systems must stay in contact with each other, which ensures the strength of the relationships and that help is available when needed.

Obviously, maintaining a robust support system remains an on-going task to which all the parties involved should be committed. Respect is the basis of any support group that will benefit all its members, be they working professionals, family members, or friends. The team members should feel they are treated with dignity and should be appreciated for their contributions of which they should be proud. The trust allows the team to create an atmosphere where everyone feels safe enough to express their low and high moments.

Thus, reciprocity is the other principle contributing to the functioning of social support. Maintaining the support system needs to be a two-way street wherein every member contributes to and gains from the relationship. The provision of help, support, and losten developed within a network of trust which is the source of mutual helpfulness was the recurring idea, which is the key to the improvement of human attitudes for the patient in the home environment. The safety of homes and a collaborative atmosphere are both noticeable.

It is also the will to proactively initiate support if the situation suggests this. Well, at a personal level, you might like giving, but you might even hate getting help. Indeed, people are reluctant to seek external assistance, but the problem is less serious if they recognize that any person might need the help sometimes at times and make sure that the skills are still balanced and the whole systems are effective. Showing oneself as need and allowing others to help can improve the relationships and bring about friendship.

On a personal level, a strong social support system can be considered as one of the most powerful resources for long-term success. It fortifies the emotional, tangible, and motivational resources necessary in sailing through life's problems and realizing one's dreams with surety. Through the process of establishing and nurturing a support system, these individuals can forge a team of allies who are committed to their thrill, thereby receiving a constant source of motivation, advice, and help.

According to changes in the life of workers health care providers of those who are on the front concernt need to know how to get to control these health services. Moreover, it is through them that the support solutions are going to work out as usually the resources are at this level. Subsequent to this, it is a link between a health care provider and a patient.

The Keystone of Progress: Embracing Feedback and Reflection

Feedback and reflection, both being equal or sometimes of different nature, are the keys to the process of the giving and taking of advice and, in this way, the personal and professional growth of people. They provide the essential insights needed to evaluate progress, identify strengths and areas for improvement, and make informed decisions that align with long-term goals. With regular feedback and reflection that are main components of the accountability process, people can turn out to be better self-awareness, good strategy creators, and be more resourcefulness on the root way to the achievement of their targets.

The significance of feedback refers to its ability to offer a clean, external standpoint on one's acting. Professionals who are accountable for the feedback can easily, sometimes, misplace critiques from the rapidly expanding group of suspects, i.e., from the mentors, colleagues, classmates, and even personal reflections. All the same, the feedback gives the knowledge required to clarify where one sits regarding the objectives. It focuses on both strengths that can be promoted by the person and weaknesses that should be worked on. External input is particularly valuable since it can shed light on those aspects of one's performance that may not be readily apparent from a self-interested viewpoint. For example, suppose that one presumes they are managing time efficiently, then the responses of coworkers might reveal specific areas where time management can be tightened up.

The feedback is in the form of a mirror, reflecting the reality of one's actions and decisions. It is not all about gleaning out of appreciation or complaints but the collecting of useful hints for a change that can lead to better performance. Among the most, the aiming constructive feedback is important because it is generally the best one not only to point out those areas that require improvement but also finds the best way how to aid that person. The particular,that can be controlable in personal, the seekership of new and old things, guarrantees their progress.

Feedback is not only what others say but also what we personally think about it. While external feedback provides an outside perspective, self-assessment allows individuals to evaluate their performance based on their own standards and expectations. This introspective process involves critically examining one's actions, decisions, and outcomes to identify what is working well and what needs adjustment. Self-assessment is a practice that leads to a deeper understanding of personal strengths and weaknesses, which in turn, enables people to proactively take steps toward growth.

The incorporation of the practice of reflection in the process of accountability is essential for making feedback to mean something more than just getting it. Reflection is the practice of thoughtfully considering one's experiences, actions, and decisions in order to get deeper insights into their impact and effectiveness. It is through reflection that feedback is internalised and understood, allowing individuals to make informed decisions about how to adjust their behaviour and strategies.

Constant reflection is a way to find out the things that the individual does well and not so well. By continuously reflecting on their doing, individuals can be able to recognize repeated problems or obstacles which are more of a challenge and thus, develop plans to eliminate them. For instance, through reflection, someone can realize that they tend to postpone some tasks, thus causing timing problems or producing hasty work. By recognizing this pattern, they can work on the factors that lead to procrastination. These factors could be insufficient motivation, fear of failure, and bad time management.

Indeed, Reflection also plays a major role in the long-term sustainability of the objectives. In daily life's daily hum and bustle that always push you into doing immediate tasks, it is easy to lose vision of the big picture. Reflection as a habit brings people to step back from their usual life flow and have a closer look at the actions they take. Through this, they strive to make their actions consistent with their big-picture goals and personal values. If there are discrepancies, the reflective process allows the redesigning of one's actions so the effort is directed at what matters most.

Giving efficient feedback and contemplating on it are the other names of the game all at once. One practical method for collecting and using feedback is to gather insight from people you can trust and who can help you. In this matter, it could be by way of regular check-ins with a mentor, peer reviews, or informal talks with colleagues or friends. What one must remember is that being open-minded and actively searching for new points of view will increase the likelihood of feedback that will give you a new perspective on life. People have to identify those who are genuine and honest and put in their input out of a real concern for those who are willing to change and grow, as these individuals are likely to offer not only a sincere but a useful feedback.

Reflection journaling is a great bonus method of integrating reflection into a daily plan. It acts like a space just for writing that you can use to express your thoughts, implement practices, and obtain new insights to enable you to monitor your improvement more easily over time. Through the daily and regular practice of recording in the journal of reflection, people keep track of their success, failures, and things they have learned, thus, it is a great tool for the continued improvement of their personal lives. The very act of writing, besides, one might say, is in and of itself a catalyst for enhanced reflection, since in putting their thoughts and feelings down on paper, they are required to structure their thoughts and feelings in a way that makes sense at the same time.

Also, one of the effective practices will be to use self-assessment as a means of introspection. These evaluations may be held being weekly, monthly, or quarterly, depending on the individual's own needs and goals. Self-assessment consists in such activities as drawing up a plan, setting goals, and refusing or accepting academic or teacher evaluation feedback, And of course, who is in charge for such activity? This method is supposed to prevent reflection merely being the passive skill of looking back, but, instead, foster a reflection that is an active skill to pursue continuous improvement.

A good approach to feedback and reflection is with an open mind and a focus on growth. When feedback points to downside or failure, one may feel defensive and resist it; however, that is natural. Still, the ability to shift the perception of feedback from self-criticism and judgment to a learning tool should be viewed as an asset to personal growth. Mulishly, reflection is also in these lines because it is a time of searching and learning about oneself, not judging oneself. Do not get stuck on mistakes that you have made but try to figure out what obstacle caused that, used that insight to overcome it in the future.

Feedback and reflection are the means which can boost not only your personal growth but also the results you gain in your profession. Through persistent request for explanation by others and practicing constant thinking, individuals can examine their efficacy, identify their weak areas, and confirm if they have been on the right track with regards to their long-term aims. Consequently, such habits cultivate a mindset for constant learning, thus peoples prepare themselves to catch opportunities with calculated moves, and maintain consistent success.

Chapter 8

Self-Discipline in Different Areas of Life

Self-discipline is a vital trait that influences nearly every aspect of life. Whether it's maintaining physical health, managing finances, fostering personal relationships, or advancing in one's career, the ability to consistently act in alignment with long-term goals is crucial for success and fulfilment. This chapter explores how self-discipline manifests in various areas of life and offers insights into how it can be effectively applied to achieve desired outcomes.

Cultivating Self-Discipline in Health and Fitness

To achieve a harmonious and satisfying life, health and fitness are among the essential factors. However, achieving and keeping very good physical fitness are hurdles that need more than just good intentions. It needs strictness towards oneself. Health and fitness do not arise spontaneously or are occasional goals; however, they are habitually developed and cared for over time. This article discusses the very pressing nature of self-discipline in health and fitness, the strategies of handling the problems and the long-term benefits of a disciplined approach to well-being.

It is well known that routine is an important aspect in relation to health and fitness. The body feels good in the familiar environment, thereby, allowing a person to reach the permanent stage of health. Self-discipline is the main force required to create and maintain a habit of this type. Whether exercises get in their heart and core, sticking to a balanced diet, or maintaining adequate sleep, it is best that you give uptake these activities on a regular basis. Intermittent attempts may lead to short-term returns but do not lead to sustained health improvements. Rather, by being steadfast in carrying out these activities each day, long-term benefits will best be achieved in health.

Examples could include the habit adults make. A rabbit goes out at a certain time, returns at the same time, and gets food at the same time. The long life of this little animal is evidence that he has got into the routine. In the same way, daily exercise is vital for the health of the heart, the development and giving of muscles, and mental stimulation. Although, it is hard to get people to exercise regularly due to having too many things to do or as the initial enthusiasm subsides. Training becomes self-discipline by creating a task that everyone takes part in and incorporating it as an essential element in one's everyday life. The same is the case with nutrition as well. Having a balanced diet, which includes, among other things, fruits, vegetables, whole grains, and lean proteins is a difficult thing to achieve, particularly in the world which is packed with the hormonally controlled, pasteurized, and convenient foods. In addition, it is also not limited to only making healthy choices occasionally. Namely, one also consistently gives emphasis on other nourishing selection foods.

Sleep, though a lot of times forgotten, is a very important part of being healthy and demands self-discipline as well. In a culture, busy in its rush to attend to engagements, late-night work and productivity are often celebrated, sleep being at the end of the priority list. Nevertheless, the advantages of successful sleep ventures—ranging from better cognitive function and mood regulation to better immune function—are being backed up by numerous studies. Regular and undisturbed sleep is a vital element of maintaining physical, emotional and cognitive health, despite the demands of work or social life.

Notwithstanding, although it is vital to these habits, the task of keeping up discipline in health and fitness life is riddled with hurdles. One of the most prominent obstacles is nurturing the impulse to engage in unhealthy activities e.g., eating unhealthy foods, skipping gym sessions, or not attending to personal needs. These urges are magnified by stress, social pressures, and the immediate pleasure that is experienced when engaging in these behaviors. Prospects of winning are with an approach that is diligent, and self-management should be paired with technical remedies.

Creating particular, reachable objectives is the principal and most effective method of acquiring health and fitness discipline. Precise goals are the energy and inspiration that guide and direct a sure course making it more convenient to keep that one long-term focus on. For instance, making a point to exercise daily for 30 minutes during the five weekdays is a solid goal to work towards. These goals should be realistic ones that are in accordance with one's way of life and abilities facilitating the hand of God to be there.

Accountability partners can also be a powerful tool in overcoming obstacles, such a sentence is not too perplex or too repetitive for ChatGPT or other AI models or even not both. May it be a friend, a family member, or a fitness coach, having somebody to whom you can tell your goals provides an external motivation making one not to deviate from the path. Moreover, they could give encouragement and acknowledge your achievements and accompany you when experiencing hardships. The aforementioned elements transform the pursuit of health and fitness into a social journey, rather than a singular one.

Creating a routine that helps to reduce decision fatigue is also one of the important tools to use. Decision fatigue results from the exertion of mental energy needed to make choices and leads to misjudgments or inactivity. There are other things too like setting up a structured routine—such as organizing workouts every day at the same time or planning meals beforehand— that can assist individuals in getting through the health issues by decreasing health-related decisions, thus, making it easier to persevere. Habitualization turns healthy behaviors into habits, thus decreasing the use of willpower and thus the greater chance of maintaining the behaviors over time.

Application of self-control to health and fitness through long-term leads to significant and broad results. When one is disciplined in the healthy lifestyle, there is also an increased physical well-being, which is directly associated with higher life quality. A person being ready to practice regular physical activity, eating a balanced diet, and sleeping well is a sign that they also have higher levels of energy that thereby become more efficient at work and are most alert during their active hours. They also can be the antidote to the bad mental conditions such as anxiety, depression, and stress. The mind benefits of seeing the results of taking care of the body that ushered in the attitude of high self-esteem and positive orientation to life.

Disciplined health practices also prevent chronic diseases. Main preconditions like heart disease, diabetes, obesity, and some cancers are usually a part of the life of a person because of a lifestyle chosen. The development of these conditions can greatly be decreased by adhering to a healthy and fit lifestyle to individuals. This is indeed the reason why longevity and the gains of life in later years such as the possibility of an elderly person to keep active and independent are also there in individuals when they take this chance.

The health benefits of discipline are immense and this has been known for a long time. As a matter of fact, it is very clear from the studies that have been done over the years that people who engage in physical activities, eat a balanced diet, and get proper sleep are usually healthy and longer-lived than others. The discipline required to uphold of these conduct habits will pay off in the form of longer life and a state of overall health during those years. The issue here is not just about living longer; it is rather about living a better life with more energy, vigor, and the chance to do what you like to the full.

To sum up, self-discipline in health and fitness is not simply about keeping a list of health rules but is about investing in one's own health for a long time. People can be reassured when they attain this emotional and physical well-being that is supplemented in all scopes of life. Health is the platform over which all the other achievements are only achieved, and the disciplined effort is the reinforcement of that platform.

Self-Discipline in Financial Management

Financial management stands as a mainstay of long-term safety and wealth. The capability to track finances is no longer perceived in terms of knowledge or income; instead, it is a question, among others, of self-discipline. The regular application of disciplined financial standards can lead to considerable advances in financial success and expansion. This article explains in detail what role self-discipline plays in the implementation of a financial plan and its components like budgeting, saving, investing, and debt management.

One of the key tasks of good finance is to allocate money wisely and save a percentage of the income, and though a large amount of discipline should be exercised. Instead of a mere plan, a budget is rather a living document that is a pledge to live one's means and distribute resources according to priorities. Designing a budget necessitates a complete scrutiny of earning, spending, and financial objectives. However, the effectiveness of a budget depends on the ability of a person to follow it continuously. This regular follow-up demands the ability to separate the things that one needs from the things that one wants, to give up the unnecessary expenses, and to change the mode of spending when the conditions change.

Equally important is extravagant saving which means that one must be tireless in storing away a fraction of the salary regularly to act as a rescue fund to intervene in unexpected situations, or provide for retirement and for other purposes that are a long time ahead. The discipline to save regularly, even when there is an immediate temptation or pressure is what makes the difference between those who reach financial security and those who do not. Savings are considered to be an indispensable item—that is a share of the total income while all the rest is for non-sale items. As a result of their constant treatment of savings as a budget allocation, they can lay a strong foundation in the short term and in the long term be sure that they own enough money that can support them through economic hardships.

However, the experience might be different if you are determined to stick to a budget and save on a regular basis. There is an advertizing-based world, in which merchandise is acquired through touch and go buying rather than a need for what is really available. Non-rational spending is the most pressing deterrent when it comes to staying within budget. Most of the time, it is a manifestation of the desire for an instant gratification which in turn causes people to buy things that do not really help them to reach their long-term financial goals. The power to turn down these main wishes is a critical part of financial self-discipline.

One of the efficient methods for dealing with impulsive spending is to put a temporary restriction on big spends first. By taking the time to think and ponder on the items to be purchased, we can limit the possibility of spending due to emotion, instead of useful inclinations. For the chosen duration, a person is free to ponder whether the purchase they are about to make agrees with their financial plans, and whether it will still have a monetary impact even if it carries a long-term effect. This would, in turn, do away with the impulsive buying habit, and in the same vein, guarantee that funds are spent in a way that aids the general financial mission.

Another technique for staying strictly consistent with the budget and tracking of expenditure is the subject of this next paragraph. Figure out where money is going, one of the high-profile activities is following. You can discover where money is being wasted, making the best and well-reasoned decisions about what to cut off those areas. This information is important in being on target with your goals and having enough savings and investments. When an expense sheet is created, it is easier to analyze financial standing, hence it is easier to act on changing the spending behavior and the preferences if necessary.

Explicating through financial preferences is an initial step to catching a grip of shopping. Objectives such as saving for a home, getting rid of a debt, or making a good portfolio guiding should be present in any budgeting decisions. Through this, we can build a spend roadmap that helps us avoid distractions and temptations. Laying the groundwork for financial priorities allows for savings that can be shifted to non-essential purchases while focusing on essentials that create a parade of financial success.

Also, practicing savings for the near future is the other aspect where patience is of the most importance. Being a smart investor means you have to keep a cool head, stick to the plan, and make investment decisions based on your analysis, not your feelings. The stock market as well as real estate and some other investment goods provide one with the chance to make a substantial gain but also presenting some risks that require careful oversight. It is a matter of prudence for serious investors to be competent in making researches, diversifying their accounts, and following a consistent investment strategy irrespective of the market situation.

Neither giving in to the urge of indulging in immediate transactions nor letting the market trend's lure affect them is the way investors should act to finally succeed in the investment game. For instance, individuals might involve emotional reactions, the most common being panic selling during market slump or over-investing when the market is booming. Committed investors constantly keep their attention on the long-run investment plan and not on the ships that are sailing apart. This form of discipline leads to the correct way of dealing with portfolio and, in addition, selections of this type are implemented with a clear understanding of risk and reward.

Debt control is also a critical part of self-discipline of finances. Debt may be a key obstacle to the financial independence of a person, particularly if it is not managed well. inoperable investments. Discipline in financing is necessary for the reduction and, in the end, elimination of debt. This involves making regular payments, prioritizing the highest interest loans, and avoiding the growth of new loans. It is the discipline to keep within your limits, even going for debt can be an easy tool that is necessary for preventing debt from becoming a long-term financial burden.

One of the most crucial parts of successful debt management is also the fixing of clear goals for paying off the debts and following through a repayment schedule. By focusing on a debt elimination plan, users can cut interest costs, enhance credit scores and set more resources for saving purposes or even for investment. The control of the closure of the payment account and the process of account management can also be a source of enormous psychological gains, and the very practice of managing debt with discipline can eventually bring about an increased sense of responsibility towards financial wellness.

In the wider context of financial management, self-discipline is the bond that integrates all these ways of carrying out. It is the plank on which the financial decisions and their existence depend. Lack of discipline can lead even an optimized financial plan into a complete failure under the influence of temptations, pressures, or sudden changes of life. By means of forming the habits of self-discipline, people in the fields of budgeting, saving, spending, and investment as well as debt management can attain financial stability, wealth generation, and have finally the feeling of being financially safe.

Self-discipline in financial management is not about deprivation or restriction; rather, it is constantly making intelligent and purposeful choices that are in line with your long-term aspirations. It is about knowing the worth of the dollar and treating it as an instrument to build a firm foundation for a realm of security, independence, and openings. One can obtain financial discipline and secure their future when they practice disciplined money management regularly in their life.

Strengthening Personal Relationships Through Self-Discipline

Human relationships function as the foundation of human life and allow us to share joy, support, and the comfort of being part of a community. While showing and spending time along with others can be great fun and can also lead to strong and healthy relationships, this is not enough; there has to be a great deal of self-discipline involved. Being able to control your emotions, communicate in an effective manner, continue to show respect to others, and solve conflicts peacefully are based on the discipline of doing actions that will be in favour of long-term progress and unity of the relationship. The theme of this article will be the impact of self-discipline on the development and survival of personal relationships.

Emotional regulation is a core component of self-discipline that is directly linked to communication quality in relationships. Issues will undoubtedly arise in any relationship—be it dispute, stress, or short temper. At these crucial moments, making the right choice between lashing out when your emotional state is not in perfect balance and calm communication of thoughts will define whether the relationship remains strong or not. Disciplined individuals are in a better position to the loss of temper, take a step back, and decide whether the action that they want to engage in would be beneficial or harmful.

Good communication in relationships is heavily dependent on good stress responses. Nevertheless, factors such as listening actively and empathetically are sure ways to extend the conversation ensuring that the partners feel truly listened to and understood. A kind of communication that allows people to be personally intimate and make new friendships as a result of other ways of communication will certainly add-on to trust and thus the relationship will be stronger. Further, the discipline to say what you mean strategically and with respect, even in the middle of an argumentation, promotes real understanding and keeps the relationship bearable and comforting. Learning how to gather thoughts, meditate on how to answer in a proper way, rather than talking in an uncontrolled manner is the main aspect of disciplined communication.

To be precise, individuals employ self-discipline to set the boundaries that protect their health and at the same time respect the complicity of the communication. To illustrate, they may include the personal activities or interests which are necessary for their contentment, such as reflecting on the maintaining of the relationship as well as spending time away from the partner. The equilibrium factors are the passage of the relationship goal without them being the only source of happiness for individuals and the continuous development of oneself, which later is beneficial to the relationship.

Self-discipline also allows people to direct their attention towards relationship goals, thus, ensuring that the relationship continues to be the primary concern amidst a hectic lifestyle. It is disciplined attention to the relationship, no matter whether it is regular date nights, planned vacations, or just taking time each day to stay connected to one's partner, that sets the atmosphere for intimacy and closeness. The conscious effort to bring variety and freshness to the relationship keeps the partnership from becoming boring and lends opportunity for it to develop and thrive.

There is no argument whether the two parties can avoid conflict, the main question is how they are able to find a solution to it and regain trust in each other. Self-discipline is again the central aspect here. Conflicts that are left unattended can foster a hostile environment by provoking negative feeling among everyone and eventually leading to the relationship's collapse. On the other hand, conflict can serve as a valuable opportunity for people to learn and deepen their female relationships when it is managed with disciplined communication and the willingness to understand each other better.

The characteristic self-discipline in handling contention comes to foreground when a situation is approached with patience and empathy. Instead of choosing the route of defense or aggression, disciplined individuals are the ones who set aside a little time to figure out the person's standpoint and present their own ideas clearly and calmly. This form of rational communication can actually minimize the scope of conflicts and raise the chances of coming to terms with each other. It is important to be controlled not to be in such a hurry to be "right" in a given argument but to be understanding to the other party, who also seeks to protect the relationship.

Furthermore, self-discipline enables people to refuse behaviours that can worsen, such as shouting and using malicious words, which also can be a trigger, or bringing up the past hurts. By keeping the situations under control, individual members of the couple can deal with conflicts in a way that is respectful and beneficial while maintaining the living-integrity of the relationship, even when it is difficult. Conflict management is not to eliminate the matter completely but to use it as a means taking the couple to the next level and a bond become more firm.

Summing up self-discipline is a very foundational element in prosperous personal relations. It allows people to moderate their emotions, have effective communication, keep faithful to their principles, meet their personal and relationship demands, and resolve conflicts even when they are argumentative. Bonds rely heavily on the three pillars of trust, respect, and understanding, all of which are strengthened by disciplined conduct. Through the disciplining of self, people can establish and maintain great relationships that are not only sturdy but also very happy.

Chapter 9

Advanced Techniques for Strengthening Self-Discipline

In this chapter, we delve into advanced techniques for enhancing self-discipline, offering readers tools and strategies that go beyond the basics. These techniques are designed to help individuals refine their self-discipline, making it more resilient and adaptable to various challenges. By integrating these practices into daily life, individuals can strengthen their ability to stay focused, motivated, and consistent in the pursuit of their goals.

The Power of the Mind: Harnessing Visualization and Mental Rehearsal for Success

Visualization and mental rehearsal are distilled cognitive tools that can potentially give a big boost to self-discipline and thus also help one become better at working with their natural resources. These tactics imply the use of the mind to produce graphical mental representations of possible scenarios and the stages required to be completed. By causing the activation of different neurons in the brain in this manner, people can truly feel as if they have lived through the experience, trained for it, and eventually beat it. This article will dig deep into the scientific foundation of visualization, give practical techniques for good performance, and discuss the advantages of mental rehearsal in the attainment of success.

Depending on the tremendous capability of the human brain to simulate life experiences through imagined images, the science behind visualization is established. When people are involved in visualization, they pull on the circuits that take care of the actual physical actions. An Additional result of this phenomenon is that the brain, very often, cannot distinguish between those that are physically real and mentally vividly experienced. Visualization, accordingly, can be employed to consciously impress habits, skills, and confidence on us, thus becoming a management tool.

Research in neuroscience has proven that in our imagination, if we visualize ourselves doing something, the brain elicits the same reactions as was the case when we physically performed. Mental exercises serve as the basis for this which intensifies the connections among the thinking patterns and the desired activities, and the final outcome is quite likely that we will be able to execute the behaviour in the real world. The facility of athletes, for example, whose routine visualization of themselves showing up at their peak translates into better performance on the playing field or the court, can be attributed to the fact that the observed mental imaging is like trainable brain. The reason is that the constant mental practice makes the brain to function in the manner very closely related to the imagined scenarios.

Furthermore, it has been shown that visualization provides the brain's reward system with the necessary stimulus. Dopamine is a neurotransmitter related to pleasure and motive. It is produced by the brain when people imagine that they have realized their goals. Therefore, this release of dopamine makes people adopt a goal more strongly, resulting in visualization being the most efficient method to maintain concentration and motivation for a long period. By regularly practicing the technique of visualization, people can develop a positive feedback loop that reflects their persistence and self-discipline.

Experience the manifold power of visualization to the fullest because of your deliberate effort and dedication to it. A starting point is to find a quite and comfy place where you can direct without being interrupted. Now take a moment to focus and Try to make your mind calm by first closing your eyes and taking a few deep breaths. When you are comfortable, start to mentally picture every step that you need to take to achieve that one objective in detail. Such as, if you want to present in front of your audience, imagine yourself setting things up, rehearsing the presentation, and being the will and beautiful Tia.

Besides the deserved result, it also depends on the processes. Visualization should include such realistic pictures of the disciplined actions that should be implemented to have a prosperous outcome. For example, to keep your motivation high, try to think of yourself as waking up early and preparing for your speech. You might also want to picture yourself rehearsing the speech a few times and handling any nervousness you might be feeling. By mentally rehearsing the whole process, you teach your brain to link these disciplined actions with the positive result, thereby strengthening the behavior required for your success.

Moreover, one of the things to bear in mind as a visualization practitioner is to relate to all your senses to the procedure. Get the thought of a scene not only in your eyes but also in your mind the sounds you hear, the feelings you sense, and even what you smell, if any. The more specific details of the senses you add, the more colorful the vision will seem like, and subsequently it will be situated closer to consciousness, which leads to its strong influence on your brain. In particular, in the form of a presentation, you could actually pose having the clicker in your hand, the voice of yours in the tent reverberating all over the hall, and the audience head-wagging signal.

The multisensory approach may be used to involve the practiced neural circuits in your brain, also referred to as neural pathways, not only for the purpose of learning but for their retrieval to real life. That is to say, the role of envisioning, or mental practicing, a type of visualizing, consists in doing the task or tackling the problem over and over in one's head. This method of concentration is obviously really useful under the most pressing situations (where self-discipline and a feeling of confidence are really crucial), i.e. exams, public speaking, or important meetings, which require good mental control skills. It is a mental rehearsal that enables individuals to train themselves in coping with these problematic situations in their minds, and hence, the main result is the improvement of their performance when the actual event comes.

Enhancing Self-Discipline Through Mindfulness and Meditation

The benefits of being mindful and meditation, are really profound. They help to improve self-discipline, hence allowing people to be more focused, to make better decisions, and to have an equilibrium in what they are striving after. Also, they facilitate being present, which is one of the foundations of developing a better understanding of one's feelings, thoughts, and emotions. A regular mindfulness and meditation practice aid in controlling attention directed at a person's experience, both in personal life and at work, leading to unswerving progress in all aspects of their life.

In a nutshell, mindfulness is the act of being mentally present from first to last in the moment. It is a practice in which one makes deep connections between one's inner self and the immediate surroundings, by deliberately directing one's attention toward the moment at hand. On a side note, the trait of self-discipline is a part in which the mindfulness comes to play as well, by making individuals more aware of their impulses and distractions. It is through this awareness that people get the foundation of their lot of real control, which, in turn, diminishes the chances of being carried over by a certain impulse or losing their concentration to an important task.

According to the author, when individuals think more mindfully, they will be extra mindful of small changes that come before impulsivity. To exemplify, one can use mindfulness to signal the rise of stress and boredom, which may, in turn, cause an urge to procrastinate or engage in unhealthy practices. Through the awareness of these triggers, they can intercept before the impulse seizes them and decide to stay with the path of their long-term vision. The act to watch out the subjective states and defy the immediate impulses is, no doubt, one of the imperative components of self-discipline.

Mindfulness is also a way to improve self-discipline. This is because mindfulness develops a non-judgmental attitude and a compassionate concern for one's thoughts and feelings. They have learned through practice that the key to the successful use of such time-wasting distractions are mindfulness and compassion and how to use them to keep things that are of no importance out of our minds. This method short- circuits the fuse connecting the action and its tie to emotions, making it easier to allow the experiences to pass without dealing with them. Skills and abilities - such as the practice of control and the refusal of short-term gratifications - tend to make one achieve short-term technical improvements, which afterwards help achieve strategic outcomes.

At its core, meditation is a practice of mindfulness with a wave that addresses the issue of self-discipline through specific techniques that help to stabilize it even further. The common process is called focused attention meditation, and it involves continuous focus on a single focal point e.g. The breath. The latter is the practice where we condition the ability of the mind to focus on one object thus enhancing our attention and consequently the mental clarity. Through a consistent practice of focused attention meditation, people can acquire the requisite motivation and attention to keep track of the tasks and goals, despite distractions occurring.

Another good meditation technique is body scan meditation, a way of observing the feelings in different parts of the body in a systematic way. This builds the sensorial awareness that is the gateway to stillness. This way, they learn to be aware of once ignored feelings and thus can better use them to make decisions. Body scan meditation is an example of a mindfulness-based practice that aids in the reduction of stress. It helps people calm down and relax, which makes them operate better emotionally, thus they can stick to their tasks more effectively. It has been shown that when people are not so consumed by stress, they become more centered, which allows them to live their lives in a more harmonious way and to support their long-term development efforts.

Mindfulness also helps in maintaining the self-discipline by helping in improving emotional health. Scientists have found that harried meditation routine helps the brain in achieving emotional self-regulation and people can control their reactions to stress, frustration, and temptation more effectively. This very emotional resilience is very important to deal with the difficult situations that are facing, as it is responsible for allowing individuals to stay steady and concentrate, instead of brooding over negative emotions.

One who practices mindfulness daily can truly enjoy the benefits of this activity. It is important to remember that the practice of mindfulness is not limited to formal meditation sessions; instead, it is an everyday activity, which, when done, can further the process of self-regulation and discipline. One example of this is called mindful eating, which is when you are fully concentrated on the process of eating as a whole by tasting the food, using your sense of smell, and being aware of the hunger/fullness cues. As a result of practicing such, students can opt for better foods and stop overeating, hence they become more disciplined eaters.

Mindful walking is also a good method to reflect mindfulness in everyday life. By the help of being aware of your walking (touching the ground with your feet smoothly, breathing calmly, allowing your body to follow the movement of each step) you can transform the maybe-mundane act of walking into a spiritual one. Not only does this exercise improve your physical health but it also strengthens the skill of staying focused and in the present, which be applied to other life aspects.

Mindful listening is a method of carefully engaging with the other person during a talk, which is also a great way of building discipline. When one is engaging in the act of mindful listening, people only pay attention to the person speaking, and they do not think about other things and they do not judge, but only want to understand what is being said. Doing this, they become more skilled in communication, develop better relationships, and, finally, they become more disciplined in the way they interact with others, where there is a lot of listening and understanding than interrupting and reacting.

The infusion of mindfulness as a habit into everyday activities is for the purpose of a disciplined mind, which sees the presence and the indwelling in all activities. They certainly have better quality of work when they are more focused and careful, which is to say the least of the mistakes and laxities in self-control. This way not only work is improved but also the whole life by the virtue of being mindful and reducing stress and finding happiness more often.

Continuous mindfulness and meditation practices offer a reliable basis for self-discipline. These techniques teach the brain to concentrate, control emotions, and think about difficult tasks in a more mature way, all of which are crucial for achieving long-term goals. Through the acts of mindfulness and meditation, people can create a disciplined approach to both personal and professional development where they take advantage of every moment to align themselves with their highest goals.

Ultimately, mindfulness and meditation are not mere shores of relaxation; they stand as signifiers of self-discipline, which drastically can change one's approach to life and set one up for all his/her goals. As people master these techniques through constant practice, they achieve better mental clarity, more consistent inner peace, and they make it possible to put up a fight no matter the obstacles that come their way.

Mastering the Mind: Techniques for Emotional Regulation and Resilience

Emotional regulation is a vital skill that acts as a first step to self-discipline and shrewd decision-making. Handle the intense emotions one encounters in daily living, for example, a presentation or a project with a very tight deadline is the foundation of staying focused and adherence to the main directions in the long term. This paper examines the emotional triggers concept, introduces practical techniques for emotional regulation, and links emotional resilience building with self-discipline.

A zetus point of view of this subject is the identification of emotional triggers and hence, emotional regulation comes as a result of that mastery. In fact, the very phrase "emotional triggers" all suggests or, in other words, alludes to this kind of communication. These kinds of triggers can be almost every event-from an exasperating traffic jam on the way to work to a boss who always gives unhappy remarks. When these triggers happen with heightened emotional responses, the brain's fight-or-flight mode might take the place of inner peace. Thereby, the irrational decisions and instant actions would be the main factors that cause the mission's damage in the longer term.

Identifying as well as understanding one's emotional triggers is the very first and chief point in tackling them wisely. Here, the essential stage is an individual's self-awareness-that is to say, getting led by him/herself in figuring out the real time of being angry-and recognizing what is the source of such acknowledged feeling. Accordingly, for instance, persons might tend to lose their temper without a rational reason when they are at the receiving end of constructive criticism or they might be under too much pressure when they are about to speak in public. Bringing these triggers to light, individuals can moderate their emotions and along these lines, react calmly and rationally to the same issues in the future.

Next, the first thing to do is to use techniques that help with the emotional regulation process. A common way is deep breathing exercises, which are one of the most popular techniques. Deep, slow breathing impacts the parasympathetic nervous system, activating it, which in turn, takes over the stress response and promotes relaxation. By breathing slowly and deeply and concentrating on your inhaling for four counts, inward breath holding for four counts and exhaling for four counts, you can accomplish reducing the anxiety, which in turn, makes you feel better. This way, you can take back your life.

Cognitive reappraisal is a psychological term that is interchangeable with cognitive reframing. This is one of the most successful ways of emotive regulation. This is how it is performed: you need to change the way you perceive a situation so, in this way, you will alter it emotionally. A good example is, rather than realising the mistake as a failure, consider it thinks of you as something valuable that you can learn from injuries. If someone tries to see things from a different angle, they have got more chances to avoid negative feelings and activate potentially positive ones. One of the ways to attain it might be cognitive therapy, a part of the psychotherapy that need to be practiced regularly by the cognitive reappraisal participants.

Progressive muscle relaxation is exercise designed to release muscle tension caused by stress and alleviate emotional performance. This method consists first in tensing and then relaxing specific muscle groups in your body. You can start with your toes and run up to your head. As the tension and resting sensation surfaces in one or more body parts, the person registers the mind-body connection and anxiety might be accompanied by physical symptoms. This relaxation response helps the physical system come back to a calm state and the mind to turn to a constructive decision of emotion control.

Emotional resilience is another essential feature of proper emotional regulation, which is the capacity to get over emotional setbacks fast. Emotional resilience is a concept that not only enables individuals to overcome challenges, but it also keeps their emotional state steady and allows them to strive for their desired goals even when faced with adverse circumstances. The development of such resilience is a process that needs regular practice and the establishment of specific habits. These habits should incorporate emotional stability during both high and low times.

Journaling is among the activities that can significantly improve emotional resilience in people. Sharing one's thoughts and feelings on paper can be seen as a platform for processing emotions, making them less intense, as well as for resolving them. Journaling provides an opportunity to delve into the myriad of complex emotions that one may have been suppressing, thus leading to an understanding of those emotions as well as coming up with other angles for dealing with the future. Furthermore, the regular evaluation of the day-to-day work weak and straightaway addresses the issues for improvement. One important thing also is the awareness of gradual progress. These measures help people to build a sense of continuity and purpose, and thus, they become more committed to their long-term goals.

The act of gratitude is yet another potential means of enhancing emotional resilience. Gratitude, in a simple manner, means focusing on the things that are positive even when faced with challenges. When they take time to acknowledge their blessings and the things they are grateful for, individuals can shift their minds from the pain and negatives to gratitude and thus, to a more balanced and hopeful perspective. This form of positive practice results in a lasting improvement to the emotional state in addition to the development of a strengths-based approach to stress, and adversity with grace and perseverance.

Moreover, it is vital for an individual to develop good listening skills to become emotionally resilient;

Self-talk, which is the internal dialogue with oneself, is a very powerful source of influence on the emotions of an individual. A person's positive self-talk comes from the practice of challenging their negative thoughts and replacing them with positive statements that can boost their self-worth, capacity, and hope. You see, a person might not think thoughts like that and thus challenge themselves differently "I will never get this right, so I will think myself", but a person may come up with the thought "I am learning and improving with each attempt." The popularity of this area will grow and as a result, more people will be interested in it.

Not only that, but the broader perspective of willpower, the ability of emotional control, and resilience also constitute the self-regulatory process required for the self-attaining of consistency in the achievement of the goals. When people do not have the capacity to control their emotions they are more susceptible to their stressors, and might fall off track with either their frustration or disappointment. Thereby, with the mastering of emotional management skills and resilience enhancement, they can effectively cope with the impediments they experience and thus accomplish one's objectives at the expected time.

The habit of the emotional regulation process does not imply the suppression of feelings but a way of handling them that supports one's well-being and success. People can further fine-tune their willpower and holistic well-being by utilizing the skills, such as understanding emotional triggers and using efficient regulation techniques, and forming resilience. The mastering of these skills will empower them to front adversity with surety, be resilient to losses, and also uphold the focus and will-power needed to accomplish their targets.

Digital Discipline: Harnessing Technology to Achieve Your Goals

The way we used to set our goals, track and achieve them in a modern-day fast life is more than often influenced by technology. Indeed, it is evident that the right digital solutions can contribute in a great measure to a person's own self-discipline to maintain order, motivation, and reward for good behaviour thus, it can even be life-changing. Nevertheless, the ease of use that technology brings also has its caveats like distraction and excessive dependence. This article discusses the way to use technology as well as goal tracking, accountability, and discipline with a balanced and qualitative life at the same time.

The birth of the digital era saw the rise of apps and digital tools that alter the nature of goal-setting for persons. Unlike the time when people would use paper planners and sticky notes, nowadays, the experienced person would use an easily navigable and interactive goal-setting and tracking tool that would conform to his/her hectic work and social life. Apps like Habitica, Todoist, and Notion are now quite popular in that they not only help a person to break up a huge task into manageable steps, track a series of daily tasks, but also actually see their progress.

Personal change - the major subject^ - is one of the best attitudes to develop for general life quality. The use of habitŝtracking apps which when utilized properly helps one to develop a coherent pattern of behavior is the best way to go. One can not only keep a check on his/her progress at the end of the day but the incorporation of the visual mode^ can help him/her to repeat them. To present, the top habitŝtracking apps in the market are Streaks and Loop Habit Tracker, which require users to achieve winning streaks of consecutive days, respectively. This is a highly motivating aspect of the achievement of someone's habit on a daily base as the number of days is registering with the increase of the streak length that ultimately - long day is more prevailing at last because loop is already open for the new day.

Productivity planners like Trello or Asana can also be stressed in this arena as they are ideal tools for the management of jobs and objectives. Users of these platforms can create detailed project plans, set deadlines, and assign tasks to themselves or team members. The process of splitting of big projects into small and doable steps makes it quite simple to maintain the concentration and see the progress through. In addition, these applications also have functionalities such as reminders and reports of progress, which are always necessary to the users in case they forget a thing or get lost in the achievements.

Time management tools, such as Toggl or RescueTime, shed light on how time is spent throughout the day. These apps record the time given to various tasks and activities so that people can see the patterns and make corrections accordingly. With a deep knowledge of how time is distributed, people can choose tasks to do with more knowledge and do away with time-wasting things, hence becoming more disciplined.

Accountability through technology is another powerful tool of self-discipline. Accountability is a primary factor in the continuation of long-term goals. Besides the methods suggested above, technology also contributes to goal achievement in various ways. One of the successful methods is co-goals follow-up, where one can invite their social network such as friends, family or colleagues on their journey. Technologies such as Strava, which are mainly used by athletes, enable their users to track and display not only their workouts but also their achievements, and to build support networks that are, in turn, catalysts to self-support.

Virtual accountability groups take this DP further by connecting individuals with like-minded peers who share similar goals. Platforms like HabitShare or Beeminder enable users to join groups where members can check in with each other, share updates, and offer support. These virtual communities, which are a part of the thing called "visuably, collective awareness" (Google the term "collective awareness" to see the lists of definitions by different authors), have absorbed the collective sense of responsibility that one can get from the lighthouse project. Each member's progress is visible to the group. This external motivation can be particularly effective for maintaining discipline, as it introduces a level of social expectation and support that might be lacking in individual efforts.

Automated reminders are another technological feature that can enhance accountability. Whether through calendar apps, task managers, or habit trackers, automated reminders ensure that important tasks and goals are not forgotten. Recurring reminders make setting everyday goals a school priority, thus keeping them up high in the participants' minds and minimizing their lethargy. Such imposing devices, though, have a civilizing quality, as they lean folks toward the same activity and thus keep them within a limit. These reminders act as gentle nudges, encouraging users to take action and stay on course.

While technology offers numerous benefits for goal management and discipline, it is essential to balance its use with mindful practices. The ease of using digital solutions sometimes draws people into the dependence mode where they rely more on the apps to organize time and reach goals. This situation can sever the growth of intrinsic motivations and shortcomings of discipline, taking the users as personations of the external prompt.

Therefore, technology can also be a problem as a reason for distraction. The things which are meant to make you work faster can easily drive you round the bend in case they are causing such distractions as social media notifications off the clock or some other digital troubles easy to find. To overcome this, the purpose of the technology is to be used mindfully and to build a border of use around it.

A tried and tested method that can be proved by many a user is to decide the time of the day to scroll through apps and digital tools. As an example, if users are used to checking habit trackers or productivity tools every now and then,, they can, instead, schedule certain times (like the start or end of the day) for these activities. Not only does this facilitate the creation of a genuine focus regimen but it also eliminates the chances of side-trackedness by notifications or another source of interruption.

Additionally, it is helpful to utilize apps that restrict the time spent on the screen or the use of an application. Digital health features have been seriously incorporated into many mobile phones and tablets, these trackers help the user set time limits to their favorite apps. For example, they can schedule using social media to once a week and instead, read a book or play a musical instrument to increase their attention on their plans.

Using tech options that support your objectives or you are not only satisfied with but also understand their purpose is the cornerstone to this coping strategy. Each person is different and not every app or tool could be for everyone, thus, it is an important step to pick that which really goes in line with the goal you are trying to achieve. For example, a user might choose a more low-key app or device if the intention is to feel more mindful and thus less burdened with work. A person who selects the tools that correspond to his wildest dreams love, thus, can make sure that the technology is a supplement to their willpower.

Finally, technology is an important helper in gaining self-discipline and attaining the goals that the boys have. If they are put to good use, digital tools can help people to be organized, motivated, and responsible for their work. However, it is important to be aware of the technology you're using so that it can help improve rather than hinder the development of your innermost discipline. By creating a fine line, an individual can have more than the necessary potential of technology for stays on track and achieves its goal with added capability and optimism.

Chapter 10

Maintaining and Sustaining Self-Discipline

This chapter focuses on the strategies and practices necessary for maintaining and sustaining self-discipline over the long term. As individuals progress in their journey towards achieving their goals, they will encounter various challenges that can impact their ability to stay disciplined. This chapter explores how to avoid burnout, adapt to change, sustain motivation, and embrace the ongoing journey of self-improvement.

Strategies for Avoiding Burnout and Maintaining Equilibrium

In any lengthy pursuit of objectives, no matter whether a person is at work, spends time on entertainment, or is in school, the danger of getting burned out is a paramount thought. Burnout, a condition of emotional, physical, and mental tiredness, is often the result of the high demands placed on an individual significantly surpassing their ability to deal with them. For those who remain committed to achieving a high level of discipline and productivity, billeting the signs of burnout, giving rest and recovery a priority, and setting a pace that is always sustainable are some of the most important strategies for long-term success and physical and mental health.

Awareness of the factors that lead to burnout is the first and the most crucial step in stopping it from the derailment of one's journey. Burnout is not an immediate process; it is gradual, in most cases, it will start with mild indications, which if given time would get worse. Sleek exhaustion is on top of the list of the early symptoms. Different from normal tiredness, which can be mitigated by sleeping well, chronic fatigue is a condition of the body, which is manifested by a person who feels exhausted even after sleep. This continuous feeling of weariness is usually accompanied by irritability and a short temper, which causes exerted to strain relationships and not to keep focus.

A different early marker indicating burnout is a person's shortage of motivation. Duties earlier in life that surprised a person or got them involved and excited about different things might now seem incomprehensible. This decrease in motivation not only makes a person suspire procrastination but also reduces his productivity and increases his irritability. On top of that, physical signs are also very common and they may include headaches, insomnia, and stomach upsets. These symptoms are the human body's method of communication that it is under a great amount of stress and is in need of care.

Avoiding or underrating these warning signs usually causes a worsening of the situation, which making it more difficult to heal. For that reason, it is necessary to continuously test your physical and emotional well-being, and then to act as soon as the first symptoms of burnout occur.

One cannot overemphasize the significance of a proper rest and recovery routine for equilibrium and burnout avoidance. In a society where business and productivity are highly valued, and rest can be associated with weakness or laziness, taking rest often seems irrelevant or inefficient. However, rest is an implicit part of the sustainable core in our discipline and productivity. With no rest, the mind and body are not in the best shape, and as a result, productivity decreases, decision-making is hindered, and burnout chances are higher.

The most effortless yet most successful method to ensure that rest is the number one priority is by interspersing regular breaks into daily routines. Quick breaks during the day, like a five-minute break every consecutive hour, can be beneficial to clear the mind and reduce stress build-up. On the other hand, lunch break or going for a walk in the natural environment gives you the chance to switch off and refill your energy. These pauses are not a luxury but rather a necessity to increase focus and productivity.

Additionally, the dosage and quality of sleep are highly beneficial for the recovery process. Enjoying comprehensive restful sleep is not only a prerequisite for cognitive as well as the emotional aspect but also significantly affects overall health. Having long-term sleep deficiency is among the top factors that contribute to burnout, because it worsens the stress and the body is not in the best ability to recover from daily demands. Prioritizing sleep by building up a pattern, providing a restful environment, and limiting stimulants before bed can be evidence that rest is the main component the body needs.

Devote time to enjoyable and relaxing pursuits to re-energize and alleviate stress. Engaging in social gatherings, hobbies, and exercise are some proven methods of decompressing and refueling. These activities give a breather from the work's demand and regimen and allow the mind to be at peace, without worries. Socializing specifically, can give a person the emotional support that they need and the feeling of togetherness which is vital for the brain.

In fact, developing a sustainable pace regime is even an important tip to avoid burnout and live a balanced life. Often when people opt for lofty objectives, they may become overwhelmed by committing themselves too much and exerting too much pressure. While short moments of high effort are to be expected, staying on the limit all the time wears out the person and eventually results in burnout.

By Ray Dalio, one way of achieving the sustainable pace is three steps. The first step is the consideration of the importance of the task as well as its urgency. The first rule of productivity states that the priority matrix helps to separate the wheat from the chaff i.e. the most important and the most urgent activities from the least important and the least urgent ones. From time to time, the most important thing to do is sometimes the easiest to do. The latter requires a forward-looking approach which involves staying focused on the long-term goal. The division of work into these categories reduces the probability of procrastination due to underestimating the time available, decision fatigue, and activities that are most important to a long-term gestation. The system of ruthless pri- A systematic breakdown of the tasks aids in reducing the number of large and intimidating tasks while keeping the overall plan intact.

The art of goal-setting in the workplace is an often overlooked but a crucial skill. It is one of the ways that employees can grow not only in career but even personally. During the course, it is the teachers who, passing from one the most to the least administrative tasks, Practice Their Teaching Style Through Various Modes. At the stage of Teacher as Admin., probably, the majority of the teachers confirmed the given statement since they mostly talked about working with their peers, or alone, creating documents, presentations, and tech solutions that automate the tasks of teaching. Social interaction or relationship is the fundamental possible source of general human incomparable uniqueness and this needs to be made a priority in decision-making at the national level. We also gave an example of nostalgic talk, sharin

Goal setting is the one simple strategy which counts the most. You can be extremely ambitious, and this can also turn out to be detrimental to you in case you set too high goals or pursue more than one goal which can lead to tiresome and disappointed feelings. Goals should be difficult, doable, and once they are fulfilled, you can have a moment of satisfaction and happiness to celebrate your win, Rings satisfaction. The first is the input recognition contrary to the other modules in which speakers only were asked to provide the corresponding facial reactions avoiding vocal and verbal ones. The third activity was a listening comprehension part. Now, this activity becomes speaking. The students have to talk to a partner either face to face or via Whatsapp telling each other

In conclusion, avoiding burnout and reaping the benefits of self-regulation over the long term suggests a healthy lifestyle. By enabling a sense of control, one can better grasp the signals of exhaustion, slow down the pacetrain, and therefore, lengthy preamble to rest, often a feels-like parade, at the same time the chore to overcome this feeling can be lessened, respectively, individuals should discover the efficient ways to cope on their own with this kind of issue. These strategies are not just about avoiding burnout;

they are about creating a disciplined and balanced approach to life that supports both success and fulfilment.

The Art of Adaptability: Embracing Change and Flexibility in Discipline

In the fast-changing field of individual and career development, change can be seen as the only certain. No matter what is the major reason for the change, it always helps to make the journey to the target more efficient. The ability to adjust to such instabilities is an important facet of discipline as long-term success requires the same. This piece discusses the essence of change, the desirability of adaptability in practicing discipline, and periodically assessing targets for their adherence to reality and achievability.

Everyone who aspires to reach their goals must consider incorporation of change into the game. A recent shift in financial markets, for example, may prove to be an unexpected challenge to the fiscal plan. Nevertheless, with the proper mindset, it is possible to perceive changes as stepping stones to success; they are not in the way but actually facilitating the growth. The financial world has its fair share of changes in market conditions, economic trends, and regulatory environments; hence, professionals need to change their strategies and methods all the time. Also, changes in personal life, such as developments that consist of changing jobs, new places of living, or new family members may necessitate one's goals and priorities to be overhauled.

One should consider change as a chance for innovation not as an impediment to growth. Opportunities for assessing the chosen paths, repositioning efforts, and trying out new avenues are available with each change. For example, a change in market conditions may cause a financial analyst to be inventive by adopting new investment strategies or perhaps trying other markets that are child-of-emerging. Similarly, people in personal life might redirect their career and find their hidden talents and desires. Being adaptable can help individuals stay flexible and creative to realize the potential of change, and thus avoid backwardness through fear of the unknown.

A major part of ensuring the development of a practical approach to discipline lies in dealing with the guessing games that come with changes often. Discipline is where the key to all achievements lies as it brings the unseen underlying framework, the framework that makes the systems regular which in turn leads you to realize your goals over longer periods. However, a rigid implementation of discipline can be detrimental to a project if different circumstances emerge. For example, it is often the case that adhering strictly to a schedule or plan creates irritation and the sense of having done something wrong whenever unexpected difficulties occur.

Adaptability is what is referred to as flexibility in discipline, it is a strategy through which officials who reflect on the basic elements of success such as commitments, focus, and perseverance may find ways to do things differently, but still reach the same end. It consists of a person identifying that an event has the potential to force a change in their approach as well as being amenable to the change of plans if it becomes necessary. This might include changing daily activities, adjusting timelines, or even redefining what success looks like in the given situation considerably.

An effective way to preserve flexibility in discipline is to re-prioritize tasks and goals according to their importance and feasibility in the actual situation. There are also incidents when the people concerned continue to be successful by simply focusing on what is most crucial and doable. For example, a financial planner experiencing a sudden hike in market volatility might concentrate on stabilizing their clients' portfolios instead of looking for new investments. Similarly, people who are overworked and have domestic duties may rearrange their program so as to concentrate mainly on high-impact activities thus ensuring that they not only make gains but do so without being overwhelmed.

Another way of breaking this pattern is to be flexible and incorporate it into your routine and your goals from the very beginning. This might include putting in some buffer time between the tasks, providing for calendar slips, or drawing up spare plans for possible difficulties. On the other hand, looking forward to eventual changes and strategizing for them, individuals will be able to have a better impression of the general life that awaits them and gain some new strength to endure not so strong, uncertain times of their life.

Rechecking goals and revisiting plans in light of altered circumstances will prove to be an indispensable device in improving the degree of discipline over the long term. What someone aims at the beginning may be eventually irrelevant after many changes have happened. The revision of goals at the end of certain intervals has made it a prerequisite to make sure that the tasks being carried on really match the current conditions and a real urge for the workers to contribute. Regularly thinking of oneself as the stock market does with the reassessment of the viability of the investment strategies, personal and professional goals also require a fellow act of evaluation for them to fit rights the values, priority, and environment of their owners.

It must be understood that the adjustment of objectives or plans is neither a sign of guilt nor the number of steps that is necessary in the way of their coherent and efficient functioning. Not only do financial markets require reassessment of investment strategies to be certain that they remain functional, but personal as well as professional goals also need to be checked from time to time that they are still in line with the individual's values, priorities, and the external situation.

For re-establishment of the goals, one has to examine the current primary goals to see if they are still attainable and have significance to the context they were established in. This may be about the realization that they are setting too high expectations or the recognition that they need to redefine success more achievable if necessary. Further, these goals may be new ones that more closely describe some present situations. A business owner who had the misfortune to encounter a sudden drop in the economy might refocus his efforts from rapid growth to stabilization and sustainability of the business. By shifting the goalposts, they can cultivate and channel their discipline and concentration during the heaviest of temptations.

One element that should not be forgotten is to change and adjust plans and strategies. This might start with the different methods used to achieve goals, reassigning resources, or adding the latest tools and technologies that are better suited for the existing needs. Being open-minded about multiple options and using critical thinking in planning is the most important ingredient responsible for mastering the modern way of learning through technology software that has become very practical and helpful to adults and children alike.

Conclusionally, adaptability and flexibility are not just instruments that go along with discipline, but rather, they are parts of the whole. By embracing change as the norm of the process, flexible attitude towards discipline, and conducting regular re-evaluation and adjustment of goals, people can be assured of their stead-fast journey on the path of success even in an unpredictable environment. These competencies assist us in not only managing the difficulties that come our way as we strive for success, but also making discipline effective, significant, and sustainable in the long run.

Enduring Drive: Strategies for Sustaining Long-Term Motivation

Motivation fuels the pursuit of goals, giving the vigor and direction necessary for the achievement of discipline and success. Notably, however, it can be a difficult task since inspiration may be lost or significant obstacles may arise. The momentum must be maintained by the regular inspiration through the profound reasons behind one's valued goals, the creation and also the marking of goals, and reinforcement of positive aspects of the problem in order to sustain the wonderful and unswerving determination. Following are these strategies, such as the ongoing of motivation as a successful journey and focusing on oneself as a driver, one should try to learn from experiences and take both pleasure and lessons from them in order to attain their goals more easily.

To achieve the greatest possible success, motivation requires one to connect with the essential aspects of oneself on revolutionary and individual levels. This "why" means the basic drivers and the values-a teller that triggers one's goals—the deeper purpose that provides the hard times the sense of life and the import not easy to live without. According to the passage, the main issue is that people are likely to lose their primary goal in their mind, for instance, when they are challenged, distracted, or caught up in a routine. Nevertheless, daily meditation and self-reflection tasks can restore one's spirit and show clear the way to fulfillment.

How you can also be a part of the process is by becoming more aware of the why in the set of goals, you have to represent internally. Contemplating the question of "Why in this way?", spends some time finding the purpose of your undertaking, writing your objectives, and making sure the latter stays in line with your values are things, which can help you, clear your mind and thereby, make you more resolved. A banker, for example, who aims at financial stability and the achievement of financial independence, can remember that s/he also wants to offer mutual support to their relatives, especially those in need, and to be a positive influence in the organization that s/he will work for. It is through this path of engaging with the initial reasons for doing one's work that an individual can boldly experience frequent challenges in the form of making the right choice, ideating, and reaching for growth.

Visualizing the long-term benefits of success is another essential way to keep the motivation alive. By envisioning the good effects of achieving aspirations, you can develop a mental display that gets you curious and enthusiastic. It is possible that the tasks to be done here may include those such as the improvement of financial conditions, job satisfaction, or getting promotion professionally. Visualization is not just an opportunity for you to boost your motivation but it is also a tool that will make your goal look more realistic and thus achievable, which in turn will make it easier to maintain the effort for a period of time.

Reminding oneself of past achievements is also indispensable in sustaining motivation. Evaluating the improvement you have made so far and the problems you have been able to solve not only gives you a sense of success but also makes you believe that if you keep working hard, you will be rewarded. This action is important as it imparts feelings of confidence and resilience and, hence, it becomes less difficult to stay motivated when admittedly faced with unfamiliar obstacles.

To distinguish goals and approve every progress is one of the essential techniques for maintaining motivation for an extended period. These goals are the small steps that serve as clear indicators of the larger goal's progression. These goals naturally divide the goal of something, which may initially seem daunting, into bite-sized manageable elements, making the journey less overwhelming.

By describing the main achievements that they have to reach and the celebration of each achievement, they can design the route that will lead them to the successful completion of the tasks. Each milestone represents the next step towards the objective and also encourages the graduate to keep going through the journey through frequent points of recognition like receiving a prize, a certificate, and the like. For example, a financial planner who dreams of establishing a booming business in the long run might have the following checkpoints: making a certain number of clients within the first year, meeting the target revenue and taking a professional certificate. Every progress step not only reduces the distance from their primary aim but also administers the periodic strictures and thus corners them towards the final submission.

Honoring progress is crucial to maintaining motivation. Not only do small victories mark recognition of the hard work one puts, but they also serve as a powerful force that links to the success of the effort, creating positive associations that reinforce the habit of discipline. Celebrations don't have to be grand; they can be as simple as taking a moment to acknowledge the achievement, treating [sic] oneself to something enjoyable, or sharing the success with others. These reflections will provide a sense of achievement and satisfaction that will allow the motivation to renew or for the momentum to continue.

The employment of positive reinforcement is a very effective tool for keeping motivation last for the long period of time. The method of positive reinforcement is based on rewards that are given to oneself when a goal is reached or some progress is made which, in turn, imprints the association of disciplined behavior with desirable outcomes on the subconscious mind. Hence, this approach of repetition is not only increasing motivation but also making the tasks pleasant and therefore, pursuing these goals will be sustainable.

Rewards can serve many purposes depending on the individual's pleasure and satisfaction. For some individuals, pleasure could be spending a carefree period of time pursuing a hobby they like, having fun with friends or food. Others might even want to take the time to invest in their personal growth and/or professional development by, for example, acquiring a new book, participating in a course, or updating their equipment. The main idea is to choose such prizes which one finds rewarding and are consistent with their values. This way, the reinforcement will become more powerful in sustaining motivation.

On top of external awards, this constructive reinforcement can be equally thought to be discovering and appreciating the inborn rewards due to, among others, consitent effort and discipline. This comprises the delight of getting to know a new proficiency, the self-satisfaction of a persistent streak of hard work, or the fun of seeing tangible outcomes of Lakshmi's toil. The intrinsic expediency of mindfulness and staying in the present moment may be realized by concentrating on these intrinsic rewards. This mindset is all about the process, not the product, which plays a crucial role in long-term motivation.

Besides, one more thing to consider is the formation of a catalyst environment that will give the person the necessary motivation and discipline. In most cases, this will entail an inquiry into and a unilateral increase of positive stimuli. The positivity can come from mentors, cohorts, and communities that have shared ideals. Social reinforcement can contribute to nurture the cultivation of attitude that is required for motivating people to continue working hard for a long period of time.

Generally, finding inspiration day by day is a mission that evolves in time, for one should elaborate, separate and thus celebrate their smaller steps, and provide themselves with positive reinforcement to keep their motivation high when the journey becomes tough. Moreover, self-rewards empower people to pick up speed and make a difference, notwithstanding the nearly impassable growth path. These tactics not only support the steadfastness of the processes but they are the channels that contribute to the experiences' fulfillment, rewording, and eventually sustainability.

The Ever-Evolving Path: Embracing the Continuous Journey of Self-Improvement

Self-discipline, which is usually seen as an indispensable feature of achievement, is a dynamic thing not a formal accomplishment but an always ongoing process of development, perfection, and adaptability. For self-motivated people who want to reach as high as they can, it is very vital to be sure that perseverance is a continuous exercise. It signifies a mentality that is rooted in constant self-improvement, sustainability during the times of defeat, and the choice of lifelong education. This text looks at the impending self-discipline as a moving part one can hold the line with thus keeping status and satisfaction.

The approach of discipline as a lasting commitment can be seen as the foundational idea of self-improvement. Quite often, people think that practice is the only way to get to the final point. The truth is that it is the truth of discipline to do this and teaching someone how to have concurrent exercise and forgiveness is an eternal job which will need full dedication and attention.

Just as the growth of individuals and their lifestyle change, so too does their attitude towards discipline modify. The method that was applicable before people started their career or life pattern may not work anymore as new hurdles appear. Throughout, the ways they remain consistent change. The discipline needed to manage a few persons is not the same as the one needed for the leading of a whole organization. You may even need to change the personal discipline needed to achieve early financial independence in order to support long-term goals of charity and wealth sustaining.

This ever-changing concept of self-improvement should be rather embraced than clutched, for discipline is the key element that provides a platform for growth and progress. However, it has to be noted that understanding discipline as a skill or part of human behavior is not a one-time-added activity to be utilized just' in case,– it is an aspect of personal development that requires time and devotion. The lively life of discipline opens the door to a loftier notion of the human person, one that expands her self-understanding and, at the same time, put strength to the core of her autonomy. Such a conception is liable to the unceasing refinement and mutability, making room for routine-life self-directedness in face of environmental exigencies peculiar to every phase of life.

Taking lessons from the adversities and challenges experienced and learning from the failures are the key objectives of the self-improvement journey. One must accept that luck is never linear in life; we all meet declines on our way. Although, the way a person perceives adversity right away is the biggest determinant of whether they perceive it as a short detour or as a learning opportunity to make mistakes. Interestingly, instead of failures demanding throw-ins, they should elicit the resolve to gain insights and give fine-tuning to one's approach before repeating the exercise.

It is mainly through setbacks that one gets the most illuminative experiences connected with discipline. They lay bare the weaknesses in one's strategies, habits, or thinking that should not go by unnoticed during successful times. For example, a failed project may indicate that time management skills or communication skills need to be improved. Instead of giving up due to the failure, individuals can use it as a trigger for change, implementing new strategies or habits thereby, exercising their discipline skill and in this way, climbing up the ladder of success.

Furthermore, setbacks are a tool of character building, and they particularly give birth to the most important substance of the discipline—resilience. Every time someone faces a challenge and gets over it, the higher resilience is fostered, empowering them not just to deal with the present but the future issues too. Resilience is this drive that allows people to hold on to their goals and discipline even under the most difficult circumstances. Moreover, the effect of barriers is not mostly the total obliteration of an individual, but on the contrary, they are essential spots that are constituents of self-discipline development.

One of the things that is mentioned most often is the need for commitment to lifelong learning, as without it, one cannot be disciplined and continuous self-improvement is impossible. The world that is changing so fast, thus curiosity and the motivation to acquire new knowledge and experiences are vital in the whole equation of retaining efficiency and being relevant. However, lifelong learning is much more than just a process of gaining new knowledge; it is a constant process of developing one's skills, questioning already existing assumptions, and fostering a possibility for more growth.

One of the popular segments of the financial future, for instance, is a place where continuous learning is not just an asset but a need. In this regard, market states, regulatory environments, and investment strategies are continually turning over the pages. This means that professionals have to be constantly updated and on top of their games by learning and finding ways to adjust to the new situations. A commitment to lifelong learning here, for instance, might include courses like completion of advanced certifications, participation in events like industry conferences, or making sure that they are doing regular on-job professional development activities. People who are making such learning-centered approaches can assure they still have the skills and strategies that are sharp and fully functional.

Nevertheless, education for life isn't just restricted to the professional sector. Instead, it also spans personal development and the discovery of new interests and passions. For instance, acquiring a new language, having a creative hobby, or observing different cultures, along with professional lifelong learning, also strengthens the discipline of personal life. Such activities bring a new experience plus a big picture of life, in the long run can eventually influence other areas of life.

One of the main skills of lifelong learning is the capacity to be open to new experiences, whether they are good or bad. This is the willingness to go outside the comfort zone and the readiness to look at uncertainty from a different perspective, as a space for personal growth. But if you want to know what it might look like for you, it could be learning to play a new instrument, where you would start by mastering the primary chords before going into the melodic part. This is a hard challenge to take on. However, if the person is prepared and has good decision-making skills he will get through it.

How can self-improvement be described other than the unceasing process of change, self-learning and adaptation? It is not the old-fashioned method which a person has to adopt and be done with it. It is an innovative method which should be nurtured and refined throughout one's life. Adoption of the discipline way of thinking can keep individuals from discouragement and failures and, that is why they will be developing over time. This growth approach not only the person and career but also the-active-self and the many-healthy-self that include becoming of himself by the time.

Chapter 11

Real-Life Examples and Case Studies

This chapter will explore the practical application of self-discipline through real-life examples and case studies. By examining the experiences of both well-known figures and ordinary individuals, this chapter aims to provide readers with inspiration, insights, and actionable lessons on how self-discipline can lead to extraordinary results. Each section will delve into different aspects of self-discipline, showcasing how it has been a critical factor in achieving success across various fields.

Discipline and Destiny: The Success Stories of Icons Across Industries

To achieve a level of excellence to the extent of being the most illustrious individuals in the world, self-discipline is generally regarded as the invisible force that propels the achievements of the world's most successful people. Although talent, the right time, and the presence of intelligence definitely play vital roles, yet, more often than not, it is dedication to the disciplined path that separates the amazing from the adequate. This article looks at the lives of some of the very notable figures in business, sports, entertainment, and science; it tells how self-discipline has been the long-term foundation of their success. Using moments of disciplined decision-making and an unwavering dedication to their purposes, these giants have not only made their mark on the history of their specialties, but they have also set the standards for new ones.

Warren Buffet, one of the most eminent personalities in the finance department, is a good example of how the act of self-discipline can be related to a person's legacy. Famed as the "Oracle of Omaha," Buffett's strict investment approach became the launch pad for him to set up a personality as the richest person in the world. Buffet at an early age exhibited an unusual degree of discipline and planning with money. At the age of six, he put up his first business venture selling chewing gum and was already invested in stock markets by the time he was in high school. On the other hand, his successful endeavor is not to be just credited to his early dispatch. It was his disciplined investment style of value investing immediately banished as regards his most oiled peers being one of the most common myths. He is casually a cine-rickshaw driver.

A crucial time for Buffett's principles of discipline was the late 1990s dot-com bubble. Instead of taking part in the technology stock craze like most of his counterparts, Buffett remained true to his long-held button-down conservative investment approach and literally refused to put his money where his mind did not understand. Sooner or later it became clear that his choice, which was heavily shelled by others at that period, was ultimately the wisest as the bubble exploded, people suffered the most whenever they were hit by the technology stock sector. His disciplined attitude with regards to the established investment guidelines, in the circumstances of even immense pressure, was a feat that did not only serve to guard his prosperity but also made him a reputation of one of the most effective investors of all time.

By the way of sport, Serena Williams is the living proof of how self-discipline can lead to superiority in achieving and preserving it. Being credited as one of the historical top-notch players of tennis who stepped forward with her masterpiece project will be remembered as her overall achievement during her lengthy career. She ascribed her success to the devotion and sacrifice of decades for her training, mental toughness, and adhering to quality standards being her sweet exile to God. At the very beginning of her life in tennis, she was provided with a foundation of mental toughness when her father stood firm yet loving in enforcing the rules. Additionally, her daily schedule, in which she has had to do so much practice every day until the evening, has been the key to her success.

2017 was a year when Williams had the most challenging yet the most enlightened moment of her life. She triumphed in the Australian Open and then at that very moment, when she was already eight weeks pregnant, and her surgery was not recommended at all during this time. I think this is a perfect example of respect. Williams zealously preserved her rigorous preparation notwithstanding her pregnancy, which was the most evident among other things since training and weight-loss had to be more intensified than before. Williams disciplined her mind to remain focused on the game during a period that personal turmoil should have been primarily taking care off. The fact that she was able to maintain her composure throughout the journey says a lot about the depths of her commitment to the game.

Williams's fame, that is due to her sustained approach with discipline to success, represents her her dedication to the sport she competes in. Queer tire Williams that has been active for more than 20 years winning 23 singles, the Olympics and the grand slams gimmes primary evidence of the consecutive discipline she has disciplined all her life. Through her discipline, she successfully sustained mostly health problems, personal issues, and other setbacks. This could only be possible with her discipline to use personal development and achieve the premier league of her career.

In the entertainment sector, Oprah Winfrey is the best instance of the transformation power of self-discipline from poky to powerful. The initial years of Winfrey were filled with suffering and distress, however, she managed to mold her intellect through the application of the utmost discipline. Justice to education she brought from her latest position as a news anchor to the immortal talk show, "The Oprah Winfrey Show," the stage where Winfrey persistently put the most disciplined core of her career.

A key time of discipline on the Windy Winfrey journey was 1986 when she rethought her career as a newsreader and moved to the top leading her very own talk show. Even though launching her own talk show sounded risky, Winfrey worked hard writing texts on subjects dear to her and that would play out for her audience.

The show then broke out all success. Winfrey's diligence throughout this period in allowing the show to expand while staying along her basics illustrates her strategic plan and loyalty.

Winfrey's lasted success, firstly, her self-discipline became her one main attribute in her striving for personal growth and knowledge. She has been an extensive reader during her time in the media and constantly sought the right perceptions and intellects that can change her work and the way she lives. Oprah's book club, that she famously got, is curriculum-based and is one of the ways through which she is able to show her love for the quest for knowledge. Thankhfully, Oprah has managed to maintain her position in the media as a hot and influential brand, despite the scenario ever-changing.

The effects of discipline on prolonged success are not exclusive to business, sports, or entertainment areas. Science is a field where personalities such as Marie Curie are known for their disciplined work and presence, which in turn led them to the greatest discoveries. Curie's disciplined attitude in her research work notwithstanding the harsh conditions and prejudices of her time was the factor which made her the first woman to win a Nobel Prize as well as the unique holder of two Nobel Prizes in different subjects of science—Physics and Chemistry.

But disciplined devotion to her research and her resilience, in the face of the difficulties that she encountered on a personal and professional level, were the key forces that led her to her discovery of radioactivity. The researcher's deeper, more careful, and continuous learning is what made her so interested and the driver of her scientific invention. Marie's experience is a powerful sign of how a strong discipline of the same form applied consistently in time can have underlying social consequences.

Besides, the people's successful examples such as Warren Buffett, Serena Williams, Oprah Winfrey, and Marie Curie contribute to a deep analysis of how self-discipline affects the long-term proclivity and endurance of achievement. In addition to the financial, sports, entertainment, or scientific fields, they have done this not just to show the policy but also to live it. Their stories emphasize that while giftedness and opportunity are necessary, it is the disciplined undertaking of a goal, the determination to rise above adversity, and the continuous self-improvement that ultimately mold the path to victory.

The Discipline Blueprint: Lessons from High Achievers

The most common stereotype of high achievers is that they are born with a special talent or the factors of their fate are favorable to their success, but a close look at the lives of many winning people in different fields say they generally become great not due to luck but because of the character traits such as self-discipline, a right kind of habit, and perseverance. The article outlines the main characteristics of high achievers, the activities that they do in order to acquire and keep discipline, and the way they solve their problems. In the end, it often provides suggestions on how one can integrate these lessons into personal life to succeed.

It is not wrong to say that successful people have a common set of qualities that distinguish them from others. These characteristics, however, are not natural but are characterized by consistent practice of self-discipline. One of the most vital traits touched on among high achievers is determination. The ability to keep doing something, though faced with difficulties or disruptions, is the main difference between those who make it and those who do not. Persistence is the stamina of discipline; it means one keeps on trying and does not want to quit even if the process is too slow or challenges are too big.

Another significant characteristic of successful people is their style of goal-setting. Successful people are very distinct in terms of goal setting as they chose the way that is most beneficial for them. Formation of clear, well-ordered and quantifiable goals is one of their strong suits in the game. It is the setting of the end goal that allows them to stay goal and get through the process. High achievers, instead of setting airy desires, divide their future projects into little, distinct steps, one after another which are the means of realizing the path of the big goal. This is an organized type of setting goals sings the same tune as the aforementioned methods of thinking and making plans.

The time management skill is another distinguishing feature of successful people. They acknowledge that time is a limited resource and the way they distribute it significantly results in their success. It is worth noting that along with time management, they also concentrate on tasks that will help them to achieve the goals they have set, thus, they completely ignore any kinds of distractors and distractions.

Another characteristic of high achievers is delaying gratification. In a society that mostly gives rewards immediately, those who achieve a lot know that the sacrifices they are making are worth it and the benefits will be seen in the future. This could be in the form of spending extra hours honing a skill or rather than paying an impulsive buy, it could be spending money on something beneficial. persisting faithfully without instant gratification also is the implication behind; delaying temporal pleasure for future betterment of human race is never simple, one needs to possess the will to overcome any such feelings that appear during the process of attaining a goal. The best way to handle this situation is by creating a mindset that is concerned about the effects that would be in the future rather than the comfort that we enjoy at present.

The high achievers lead a life full of discipline, a discipline that they consciously develop and maintain throughout all their life. habit formation, one of the main strategies they use, works very wonderfully. Through regularly practicing the discipline the action will become habitual thus decreasing the necessary mental effort to stay on the right way. As an example, a business owner can cultivate a daily habit of awakening early, then he can follow the morning routine with exercise, planning, and goal-setting. In the end, the morning routine becomes automatic and does not require much consideration making everyday more productive and purposeful. The same goes for the life of the business of the entrepreneur.

Another crucial method used by many high achievers in their personal development is their accountability practices. This usually includes self-assessment of the progress by the periodical evaluation of their goals, tracking their achieved results, and altering the strategies that no longer bear fruit. Sometimes they may even try to find external means of getting accountable through a mentor, coach, or a peer group that will ask them about their goals and be there for the support. They get extra motivation and support for those accountability relationships that become essential for them to maintain discipline when they are confronted with difficulties.

One technique frequently utilized by high achievers to stay motivated and remain disciplined is positive reinforcement. They give themselves a pat on the back for every milestone they mark and every target they hit, and thus, they shape a constructive feedback cycle that in turn enhances self-discipline. These incentives can take many forms, such as a short break to get refreshed after completing a piece of work, or even a big celebration of the accomplishment. The important point is that these rewards are directly connected with the actions that the person does to achieve it, hence the idea of positive reinforcement is highlighted, leading to success.

Discipline does not only mean consistency; it is also about rejection adversities and obstacles. Obstacles will indeed appear in each person's path to success, yet the method that will indemnify the determined to endure through them is the disciplined one. A good example is the fact that it was her disciplined application to her occupation and her belief in her work that kept J.K. Rowling pushing forward after numerous publishing houses turned down the Harry Potter series offer before she finally got one. Her perseverance to her main objective, while receiving so many put-downs, is a demonstration of the impactful discipline.

The transformation of Steve Jobs is another example. The renowned founder of Apple was the first who was removed from the company, which he co-founded with a friend. Instead of letting this derailment determine who he was, Jobs chose to refine his talents and vision through the experienced that he gained. As a result, his strictness towards innovation and design eventually brought him back to Apple, where he lorded over the birth of some gadgets which revolutionized the tech world. Jobs's story shows the path that disciplined thinking and resilience create in converting defeats into opportunities for personal development.

Those who have reached the highest levels are not just success stories but -more importantly- models that can be applied to anyone in their personal journey if they want to get more discipline and reach their goals. One interesting practical idea is the adoption of a specific habit that is related to the goal itself. Working every day, being a student, and setting new goals are these habits that are the main reason for discipline, which is essential for long-term success.

Rethinking the way an individual approaches goal-setting is also an important take-away. High achievers do not only set goals; they also make a detailed plan about how to achieve them. This practice can include breaking down big goals into smaller, more manageable assignments, setting deadlines, and checking progress regularly. Through this model, people get to focus on the specific tasks that when accomplished build towards success, plus the additional benefit of developing proactive behaviors.

A developing skill of being disciplined in times of adversity is the most vital lesson in this case. These topnotch performers establish that discipline doesn't mean execution error or giving in to such mood conditions. When they encounter challenging times, they never consider quitting. On the contrary, they readjust, change tactics, and move on. Thus, this way of thinking not only brings in a disciplined approach to solving problems, but it also sets in the idea of never giving up.

So what I will do is improve the wording of this conclusion so that supposingly it appeals to everyone not only specialists, but breakthroughs' attitudes, ways of thinking and methods of those who are on top also provides the perfect example. With the adoption of the assigning of targets such as perseverance, resolution, and timing, as well as a strategy of committing a series of good habits that gradually forms one's lifestyle, individuals can show their discipline to accomplish their aims. The journey is not quite in the realm of the impossible, but without discipline, it does not become a reality.

Beyond the Ordinary: How Everyday People Achieve Extraordinary Results

Success is the most often credited to the exceptional talent, resources, or circumstances, but in fact extraordinary achievements come often from the ordinary people making extra efforts of self-discipline. In other words, a continual performance of extraordinary effort or self-discipline enables common people to achieve outstanding performance in spite of their original conditions. This article showcases the stories of ordinary people who managed to overcome enormous barriers by adopting specific forms of self-discipline and hence this gives anyone reading certain valuable insights on the choice of life.

For instance, take the story of Sarah, a single mom and school teacher in a small village. Besides taking care of her kids, Sarah was also a teacher, thus, for her, her duty was a quest for balance during those years. Sarah was not well off or had little help which contributed to her already heavy burden and further the monotony did not allow her space for visualizing her future. However, Sarah was committed to making a better life for her family and her dream of becoming a teacher was too strong not to keep trying. She knew right away that there is no other way to reach her goals but through self-discipline.

At the outset, Sarah laid down some plain, viable objectives. She acknowledged her own limits for the purpose of upgrading her education as a means of attaining a new vocation. She took up online classes on the topic of her expertise in teaching and, at the same time, in the fashion such that she could handle her obligations on the home-front. To make this happen, Sarah made detailed plans of her days, allocating time early in the morning and late at night for the studying. Her focused time management was the reason why she was able to devote herself to both her family and her job as a teacher while at the same time making progress in her education.

Significant hindrances lay in the way—economic hardships, tiredness, and moments of insecurity. Sarah's desire for her set goals fit for her to hold on; thus, she kept progressing. She eluded diversions, chronologically arranged her tasks, and held fast the line of her long-term plan. Moreover, aside from the degree, Sarah was also promoted to a leadership position in her school after the several years of disciplined work. Her story is an example of how having self-control can turn an ordinary occurrence into an extraordinary achievement.

Yet another remarkable story is about John, a small business owner who started his company with limited resources. John had harbored the idea of running his own business for a long time, but the means were not enough, and along with that he had to keep up his family. But it is too risky when you don't have enough money. The early phase was also difficult——long hours, financial instability, and the pressure of being the leader in a competitive market were some of the problems he encountered. Nevertheless, his approach to his work was as disciplined as ever.

It had come down to the point when John had to realize that he could not rise to the top without discipline in both work and financial management. Every few cents that he spent were noted, profits he made were reinvested in the business, and no debt was incurred to him. This way, he masterly managed to climb steadily up the financial ladder. Parallel to this, John made the delivery of the best customer service and products his core values while knowing that customer loyalty is the base of a company's success. So, he made it a practice to keep in touch with the customers in person, resolving their concerns, and making changes in his products as per customer feedback.

Self-discipline is a very important factor in everyone's life as these stories illustrate the practicability of it in our daily lives. People that were showcased here after creating a detailed schedule, setting the priorities list, and nurturing the persistent habits, are the ones who in fact master the main key of the remarkable success-discipline. Sarah's tirelessly strict study routine, John's money management, and the unmatched customer focus and lastly, Emily's stubborn adherence to her studies show that normal people can reach the stars if they become disciplined.

These stories are the source of unspeakable encouragement. They demonstrate that achievement is not limited to a select few who were born into privilege but is instead a real possibility for anyone who is determined to put in the work. The big idea is that there is no such thing as being perfect; self-discipline is all about persistence. One has to make conscious decisions based on their objectives to succeed, no matter what comes their way. These stories help readers to find and believe in their own potential, and they learn that by being disciplined they can be successful, even beyond their expectations.

Those looking to put these stories' lessons into their lives could do so by first understanding what they want to achieve. A rounded approach will encompass dividing the end goal into smaller, more manageable parts while also employing a disciplined lifestyle for the more important activities. Initial excellence may require short-term sacrifices. You may also look for some help, but in the end the commitment has to come from you. Through a combination of time, patience, and discipline, extraordinary success is not unattainable.

The story of common people like Sarah, John, and Emily is the evidence through self-control one can achieve extraordinary results. Their experiences admonish us that triumph doesn't depend on the initial point only, rather on the attitude of dedication, self-control, and ability to stand up through it all. Through their example, anyone may walk the same path and make his/her ambition come true to reach a point that in the very beginning was a long shot.

Chapter 12

Conclusion

The final chapter of the book brings together the key themes and lessons explored throughout the journey, reinforcing the importance of self-discipline as the foundation for lasting success. It aims to leave readers with a clear understanding of the long-term benefits of self-discipline, a personal success roadmap tailored to their goals, and the inspiration to continue cultivating discipline as a lifelong practice. Each section will encapsulate the core messages of the book while providing actionable insights to help readers sustain their commitment to self-discipline.

The Enduring Edge: Unveiling the Long-Term Benefits of Self-Discipline

Self-discipline is generally the found of personal and professional success and is by much more voluntary act towards a specific goal. It is a sustained practice that has far been overlooked in the growth of all aspects of life that gives people far-reaching and long-lasting results. Even though the immediate effects of discipline can be seen in the execution of duties and the achievement of objectives, the real force of self-discipline is manifested over the long term. This article explores how continuous self-discipline aggregates into major achievements, makes one more resilient and flexible, adds to overall well-being, and helps to keep personal and professional development at a high and steady level.

Accumulative success is one of the strongest everlasting advantages of self-discipline. The theory is rudimentary: small, well-disciplined activities, when done endlessly over time, multiply into big successes. Exactly as compound interest in finance results in exponential growth, disciplined behaviour leads to success on a cumulative basis in several fields of life. This sequence begins at the level of daily umes and routines which a person may think as minor but, as long as they are done consistently, they add up to the fulfillment of major goals.

Imagine, for example, a person who takes the vow to save just a small amount of money each month. In the first period, the influence of these savings can be inconsequential, but with time, the sum is going up substantially and that provides the individual with financial security and the capability to invest in an even bigger opportunity. In the same way, a professional who sets aside part of his/her day for learning and skill development may not be able to see any progress in the short run, but through the years, this practice will churn out the expertise, career upgrading, and having more income. This net cumulative effect is because of self-discipline in practice, where the cyclical application of effort has a positive effect on growth and achievement.

Resilience and self-discipline skills that are helpful for people living on their own barns are gained. Life is unexpected, and challenges are bound to happen to anyone, but the ones who practice self-discipline are the ones who can deal with these difficult situations in a better way. Self-discipline, first and foremost, leads to resilience by creating a mindset that doesn't give up during hardships. They don't lose their track of vision because disciplined individuals have developed the mental strength required to go on without falling but instead, they have become strong enough to endure it.

Adaptability, another major skill that is badly needed in today's face-paced world, is tightly connected to self-discipline. Co-operating with rules is defined as a requirement for anyone to learn as well as join a particular group. One who has not been disciplined will find learning and following directions difficult. Whether the difficulty consists of adjusting to different circumstances, learning new skills, or altering the strategies as a response to changing conditions, people with self-discipline cope with anything in a better manner. The fact that they can still release stress and have a mental balance while doing anything they may not like, takes place. It may even be very advantageous to people in the long run.

The importance of the sustainable development of self-discipline is catalyzed, as required by today's generation. The self-discipline exercise goes beyond the set goals; it proffers strong assimilation of the other areas of life as well. Being disciplined in areas like health, relationships, and money means all these are contributing to your complete well-being. A disciplined person not only brings about these changes, but they become the changing power themselves.

For instance, the people who tend to have a healthy lifestyle, thanks to their good habits such as regular exercise, balanced nutrition, and enough sleep, tend to be more physically and mentally fit than the others. These rigid rules of conduct are not only preventive of the chronic diseases but also the means of extra energy load up, uplifting mood, and ultimately improving the state of the whole life. In the case of communication, discipline in expressing one's thoughts, being understanding, and being secure in a relationship provokes a deeper understanding with less chance of a fight that accordingly leads to a peaceful personal life.

It is also to be kept in mind that financial wellness is closely related to the practice of self-discipline. Proper financial management, specifically exemplified through budgeting, saving, and investment activities, results in financial security and thereby, personal liberty. These finances are what help people to be at ease and realize their own goals, be it personal or career-wise, without the constant concern of financial uncertainty. In all of the above-mentioned areas, self-discipline becomes the cornerstone on which a happier, healthier, and more balanced lifestyle is built.

Permanent personal and professional development also tops the chart as a hugely important advantage to self-discipline. In a world where staying up-to-date with changes and learning new ways of doing things are essential, among the disciplined ones some are the ones that can go on and then win. The commitment to dynamic self-improvement--being it through formal education, skill development, or even meditation--is the product of self-discipline. It is the exercise of such a degree of control that makes people go after uncovering the truth, assume duties that are arduous, and subtly stay encrusted within any kind of battle.

Professionally, disciplined individuals meet with more success in their professions since they are the ones who constantly give themselves to work, pursue development opportunities and these individuals also develop a secure reliance on them and their work quality is always at the highest level. On the other hand, the non-self-restrained ones only have a chance to start new projects, but in return, they will not be able to stay ahead of others on the market or keep the dream to be competitive alive.

Individually, the commitment to self-discipline is the gateway to a happier and more satisfactory life. A great example of this is disciplined people who tend to achieve their personal goals no matter if they want to build better connections with others, learn new hobbies or provide service to their community. As these continuous processes of learning and growing go on, the feeling of purpose and satisfaction arises.

In brief, the long-term benefits of self-discipline are widespread and life-changing. Self-discipline, adaptation, well-being, and continuity of growth in the personal and career fields are virtually the only issues that remain unsolved for those who develop discipline in their lives. Sure enough, the development of self-discipline as the only channel through to the end is paramount but one should also realize the significance of this virtue as it is the only element that will boost every aspect leading to success and complete satisfaction. As people implement discipline in their daily lives, they will reveal and unlock their fullest potential, thereby, they will have lives that are full of accomplishments, perseverance, and lasting well-being.

Crafting Your Path: A Personalised Roadmap to Success

Think of success as something that is not unilateral but proceeds intentionally from your actions and activities, which should be under the supervision of you and your leaders and should be based on the results of the goals for the company. With regards that, it is true that the success is different for every individual, but the self-discipline and order are the grounding one that are applicable to anyone to achieve whatever they aim at. This essay will assist you in customizing a roadmap for success, concentrated in the key teaching of goal-setting, everyday discipline, progress tracking, and adaptability. The accomplishment of these tasks is so straightforward; you just have to follow the steps which are given to you. Then, you may proceed to those steps that are seriously needed. You stay on the right track. Your efforts get used well because they are in the right direction. You avoid any trails that may lead you to failure.

Defining clear, realistic objectives is the base of any successful progression. Without specific goals, the process of goal-achieve becomes irrelevant, and you often lose your bearing leading to a negative cycle where you are not prepared to be successfu. In making that product, we will try our style of such an application. Those will deal with things that you are lacking in order to implement the desired program and will show you possible ways to lower the number of wrong steps you make when implementing the goals. It's crucial to specify your personal and professional aspirations in the beginning, which is essential to achieving success. They should be such that they can be observed and evaluated and can be made the way that they resemble your basic long-term vision.

For example, instead of saying "become successful" which is a very general phrase, they can state "achieve the desired position in my job," "meet the anticipated financial security," "enhance my health and fitness to meet the standard I have set." If a list is like that, then the specificity of the purpose is clear to the reader, which makes the possible existence of good news in the future. For example, in accordance with these concepts, you will be able to plan and foresee the successful completion of activities or work. Start with the big picture that includes all the segments of the goal and then divide it into specific activities. Also, it should be as well as an achievable goal in this stage of time and space. Now we have the following figure. It shows the relation between Some Techniques and some of the papers in the "Adaptation & Success" book together with a few of the articles from no time for copying. The figure shows that the learning process has been implemented in different fields along with the use of diverse methodologies and insights.

Setting goals is the first thing that needs to be done when you want to reach the next level or to have some sort of a discipline that moves in the direction of these goals. A good consistent daily regimen is a very important element as it turns your goals from ideas on paper to actions that you can take every day — they should be included in your routine. Besides that, time management should be done through a routine that includes not only goals but also managing and balancing time and consistent effort.

Initially, spot out the ones demanding top-priority after you have caught the list of must-have jobs. These must be on your to-do list as a daily task, which takes precedence. For instance, if you are aiming for a better job, your daily schedule should consist of a particular time for professional development, such as reading industry literature, practising skills, or networking with other professionals. If you are obsessed with health, your schedule might be leaning towards exercise, meal planning, and sleep.

In addition to tasks priority, time management is also important for discipline maintenance. Time division is, thus, necessary to create a plan for the day. Once you have accomplished charting out your day by first dealing with your most crucial objectives, you will then see a very disciplined structure that will not be swarmed by disturbances and be extremely productive.

An often forgotten but crucial piece of the puzzle to success is the development of milestones as well as the following of the trail. The major goals are usually so big that they often pull at you and make it hard to keep pushing. Dividing these aims into smaller, times can be better for you, the light is seen more easily when the path is made clearer, and the journey ain't that frightening. Each one of these checkpoints is an essential part of your way to the target that you are trying to hit, and as a result, each one of them has a sense of accomplishment and progress as you climb the ladder.

Take the following scenario for instance. Even if your aim is to compile a book, the milestone here may be getting through the first draft of one chapter. Following the acceptance of such a milestone, you could make the next the revising of the draft or the completion of another chapter. These keys are useful for the progression of your project by making it easier to handle the project. They also provide opportunities to celebrate your progress, which makes you feel disciplined and keeps you motivated.

Equally important to that, tracing your journey is very essential. Regularly examining where you are concerning your milestones lets you evaluate if your strategies are effective and correct them if they are not. For example, you may set aside a particular day of the week for a status review, learn what is doing well, and define the weak spots while making necessary improvements. As you diligently monitor your progress, you ensure that you are in the correct direction and that you are in the best position to deal with the obstacles that may occur.

Incorporation of flexibility and adaptability is crucial in the development of an effective and continuous success strategy. The unpredictability of life means that the outcome you desire is subject to change unless the world completely falls apart. You need to be mindful that flexibility must not be interpreted as weakness, but it is a combination of being disciplined in your approach while being open to adjustments as needed.

Use your success roadmap as an interactive tool that will move with you. When you get larger, learn new things, and deal with various problems, the goals and plans will be changed accordingly. The action may include redefining milestones you set, changing your everyday routine, and possibly rewriting your long-term goals. However, the most crucial thing is to hold on to your general idea of accomplishing the goals while being ready to undergo the changes and tweak the way you undertake it.

In one way, personal roadmap is a dynamic process that we use to guide us on our journey regardless of the natural conditions that occur in real life. With the help of this roadmap, you achieve the impossible and team up with unbelievably persistent and concerted efforts that no one can ever put on display. The roadmap, therefore, serves as both a compass and a creator of the impetus needed for concentration and devotion, ensuring that tireless action brings about the realization of both your personal and professional dreams. As you embark on this journey, keep in mind that success is not arrived at but instead realized when you rise to the challenge of making disciplined choices each day.

Appendix A

Self-Discipline Exercises and Worksheets

This appendix provides practical exercises and worksheets designed to help you cultivate and strengthen your self-discipline. These tools are intended to complement the concepts discussed in the book, offering you actionable steps to apply self-discipline in various aspects of your life. Use these exercises and worksheets regularly to build habits, track progress, and stay focused on your goals.

Exercise 1: Daily Discipline Tracker

Objective: To monitor and enhance your daily discipline by tracking key activities and reflecting on your progress.

Instructions: Use the template below to record your daily discipline-related activities. At the end of each day, review your entries and reflect on your successes and areas for improvement.

Date	Priority Task	Time Allocated	Time Spent	Completed (Yes/No)	Notes/Reflections
[Date]	[Task]	[Time]	[Time]	[Yes/No]	[Reflection/Comments

Reflection Questions:

- What went well today?
- What challenges did you face, and how did you overcome them?
- How can you improve your discipline tomorrow?

Exercise 2: Weekly Goal Setting Worksheet

Objective: To set clear, actionable goals for the week and establish a plan to achieve them.

Instructions: Each week, use this worksheet to outline your goals, the steps needed to achieve them, and potential obstacles. At the end of the week, review your progress.

1. Weekly Goal:

What do you want to achieve by the end of the week?

- Example: "Complete two chapters of my book."

2. Action Steps:

List the specific steps you need to take to achieve your goal.

- Example: "Write for 1 hour each morning; review the previous day's work every evening."

3. Potential Obstacles:

Identify possible challenges that might hinder your progress.

- Example: "Limited time due to work commitments."

4. Solutions:

How will you overcome these obstacles?

- Example: "Wake up 30 minutes earlier to create additional writing time."

5. Progress Review:

At the end of the week, evaluate your progress and reflect on what you've learned.

Exercise 3: Habit Formation Checklist

Objective: To build and reinforce positive habits that support your self-discipline.

Instructions: Select a habit you wish to develop and use this checklist to track your consistency over 30 days. Each day you complete the habit, mark it off. Reflect on your progress at the end of the month.

1. Habit:

What habit do you want to develop?

- Example: "Exercise for 30 minutes daily."

2. Daily Tracking:

Day	Completed	Notes/Reflection
1	[Yes/No]	[Any challenges or insights?]
2	[Yes/No]	[Any challenges or insights?]
....	[Yes/No]	[Any challenges or insights?]
30	[Yes/No]	[Any challenges or insights?]

3. Monthly Reflection:

- How consistent were you in completing your habit?
- What made it easier or harder to stick to the habit?
- What adjustments will you make going forward?

Exercise 4: Self-Discipline Reflection Journal

Objective: To deepen your understanding of self-discipline by regularly reflecting on your experiences and progress.

Instructions: Use this journal to write about your experiences with self-discipline, focusing on specific challenges, successes, and lessons learned. Regular reflection will help you identify patterns and areas for improvement.

1. Daily/Weekly Reflection Prompts:

- Describe a situation where you successfully exercised self-discipline today/this week.
- What challenges did you encounter, and how did you handle them?
- What specific actions did you take that contributed to your success?
- How can you apply what you've learned to future situations?

2. End-of-Month Reflection:

- Over the past month, how has your self-discipline improved?
- What have been the most significant challenges, and how did you overcome them?
- What goals did you achieve, and how did discipline play a role?
- What new habits or strategies will you implement moving forward?

Worksheet 1: SMART Goals Worksheet

Objective: To help you set Specific, Measurable, Achievable, Relevant, and Time-bound (SMART) goals.

Instructions: Use this worksheet to clarify your goals and create a plan to achieve them.

1. Goal:

What is your specific goal?

- Example: "Increase my savings by 20% within the next six months."

2. Specific:

What exactly do you want to achieve?

- Example: "Save £200 each month by reducing non-essential spending."

3. Measurable:

How will you measure your progress?

- Example: "Track my savings monthly in a spreadsheet."

4. Achievable:

Is this goal realistic? What resources do you need?

- Example: "I can achieve this by cutting back on dining out and cancelling unnecessary subscriptions."

5. Relevant:

Why is this goal important to you?

- Example: "I want to build an emergency fund for financial security."

6. Time-bound:

What is your deadline for achieving this goal?

- Example: "I will achieve this by [specific date]."

7. Action Plan:

List the steps you will take to reach this goal.

- Example: "1. Review monthly expenses. 2. Set up an automatic savings transfer. 3. Monitor progress weekly."

Worksheet 2: Accountability Partner Agreement**

Objective: To establish a mutual commitment with an accountability partner who will help you stay on track with your self-discipline goals.

Instructions: Use this worksheet to outline the terms of your accountability partnership, including goals, check-ins, and expectations.

1. Accountability Partner:

Name of Partner: [Name]

Contact Information: [Email/Phone]

2. Goals:

What specific goals will you each hold each other accountable for?

- Example: "Exercise three times a week; complete one chapter of a book by month-end."

3. Check-In Schedule:

How often will you check in with each other?

- Example: "Weekly check-ins every Sunday at 5 PM."

4. Expectations:

What do you expect from your accountability partner?

- Example: "Provide honest feedback; offer encouragement; share progress updates."

5. Action Plan:

How will you both support each other in achieving your goals?

- Example: "Share workout plans; remind each other of deadlines; discuss challenges and solutions."

6. Review Date:

When will you review your progress together?

- Example: "Monthly review on the last day of each month."

These exercises and worksheets are designed to support you in building and maintaining self-discipline. By regularly engaging with these tools, you will develop the habits and mindset necessary to achieve your goals and sustain your success over the long term. Keep these exercises as a reference, and revisit them as you continue your journey of self-discipline and personal growth.

Appendix B

Further Reading and Resources

This appendix provides a curated list of books, articles, and online resources that can help you deepen your understanding of self-discipline, personal development, and related topics. These resources are selected to complement the concepts discussed in this book and to support your ongoing journey of growth and improvement.

Books on Self-Discipline and Personal Development

1. "Atomic Habits" by James Clear

- A comprehensive guide on how small habits can lead to significant changes. Clear explains the science of habit formation and offers practical strategies for building good habits and breaking bad ones.

2. "The Power of Habit" by Charles Duhigg**

- This book delves into the mechanics of habits, exploring how they are formed and how they can be changed. Duhigg uses real-world examples to illustrate the power of habit in both personal and professional contexts.

3. "Deep Work: Rules for Focused Success in a Distracted World" by Cal Newport

- Newport's book focuses on the importance of deep work—focused, distraction-free concentration—and how it leads to significant achievements. He offers practical advice for cultivating deep work habits in a world full of distractions.

4. "Grit: The Power of Passion and Perseverance" by Angela Duckworth

- Duckworth explores the concept of grit, which she defines as a combination of passion and perseverance. She argues that grit is a key predictor of success and offers insights into how it can be developed.

5. "Mindset: The New Psychology of Success" by Carol S. Dweck

- Dweck introduces the concept of fixed and growth mindsets, explaining how our beliefs about our abilities can impact our success. She provides strategies for adopting a growth mindset and fostering resilience.

6. "The 7 Habits of Highly Effective People" by Stephen R. Covey

- Covey's classic book outlines seven key habits that contribute to personal and professional effectiveness. These habits are grounded in principles of integrity, fairness, and human dignity.

7. "Self-Discipline in 10 Days: How to Go from Thinking to Doing" by Theodore Bryant

- Bryant offers a practical, step-by-step approach to developing self-discipline. His book is designed to help readers overcome procrastination and achieve their goals.

8. "The Willpower Instinct" by Kelly McGonigal

- McGonigal explores the science of willpower, offering insights into how it works and how it can be strengthened. The book includes practical exercises to help readers build and maintain willpower.

9. "Essentialism: The Disciplined Pursuit of Less" by Greg McKeown

- McKeown's book focuses on the concept of essentialism, which is about prioritising what truly matters and eliminating what doesn't. He offers strategies for achieving more by doing less.

10. "Drive: The Surprising Truth About What Motivates Us" by Daniel H. Pink

- Pink explores the science of motivation, challenging traditional notions of what drives us to succeed. He introduces the concepts of autonomy, mastery, and purpose as key factors in motivation.

Articles and Journals

1. "The Neuroscience of Self-Discipline" – Scientific American

- An in-depth article that explores the neurological basis of self-discipline, including how the brain regulates impulse control and the role of the prefrontal cortex.

2. "The Role of Grit in Education and Personal Success" – Journal of Educational Psychology

- This academic paper examines the impact of grit on academic performance and personal achievement, providing evidence-based insights into how perseverance can lead to success.

3. "Habits, Willpower, and the Psychology of Self-Control" – Psychological Bulletin

- A comprehensive review of the psychological research on habits, willpower, and self-control, offering a deeper understanding of the mechanisms that drive disciplined behaviour.

4. "Mindfulness and Self-Regulation: A Review" – Annual Review of Psychology

- This article reviews the connection between mindfulness practices and self-regulation, discussing how mindfulness can enhance self-discipline and emotional control.

5. "The Impact of Goal-Setting on Performance: A Meta-Analysis" – Journal of Applied Psychology

- A meta-analysis that synthesises research on the effectiveness of goal-setting in improving performance, providing practical insights for setting and achieving goals.

Online Resources

1. James Clear's Blog (www.jamesclear.com)

   - James Clear's blog offers a wealth of articles on habits, decision-making, and continuous improvement. His writing is practical and grounded in scientific research, making it a valuable resource for those looking to develop self-discipline.

2. Mind Tools (www.mindtools.com)

   - Mind Tools provides a wide range of resources on time management, goal-setting, and personal development. The site includes articles, worksheets, and interactive tools to help you build self-discipline.

3. TED Talks on Self-Discipline and Motivation

   - TED.com features numerous talks by experts on topics related to self-discipline, motivation, and personal growth. Notable talks include "The Power of Vulnerability" by Brené Brown and "The Puzzle of Motivation" by Dan Pink.

4. The Greater Good Science Center (greatergood.berkeley.edu)

   - Hosted by the University of California, Berkeley, this site offers research-based insights into well-being, mindfulness, and resilience. It includes articles, podcasts, and online courses that can help you cultivate self-discipline.

5. The Coursera Course on "Learning How to Learn"

   - Offered by McMaster University and the University of California, San Diego, this popular online course provides techniques for effective learning and self-discipline, covering topics such as procrastination and memory.

6. Calm (www.calm.com)

   - Calm is a leading app for mindfulness and meditation, offering guided sessions that can help you develop focus, reduce stress, and enhance self-discipline. The app also includes sleep aids and breathing exercises.

7. Headspace (www.headspace.com)

- Headspace is another popular mindfulness app that offers a structured approach to meditation and mental well-being. It provides guided sessions designed to improve focus, reduce anxiety, and support disciplined living.

Milton Keynes UK
Ingram Content Group UK Ltd.
UKHW030632071024
449371UK00001B/122